D1135022

Antique Silver

A guide for would-be connoisseurs

Antique Silver

A Guide For Would-Be Connoisseurs

JOHN LUDDINGTON

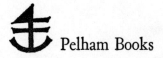 Pelham Books

First published in Great Britain by
PELHAM BOOKS LTD
52 Bedford Square
London, W.C.1
1971

7207 0497 9

Set and printed in Great Britain by
Northumberland Press Limited, Gateshead
in Granjon eleven on twelve point and
bound by the Dorstel Press, Harlow

This book is dedicated to all those collectors and dealers who still feel the need of a guide to hall-marks before they can ascertain the approximate date of an article of antique silver. It is also dedicated to those who feel they have nothing left to learn about silver.

Note: Dedicatees will find an explanation to the above in the pages of the book.

Contents

List of Illustrations

ILLUSTRATIONS IN TEXT

Foreword

John Luddington has written a most valuable work on antique silver and its pitfalls. His carefully constructed analyses should assist both collector and dealer alike. Coming at a time when 'teach-in' and other 'crash-courses' on the subject of antiques have become the vogue, a written course for the beginner will be most gratefully received.

Mr Luddington, fearless dealer that he is, has elected to deal with such dangerous subjects as 'forgeries', 'confidence tricksters', and has even attempted to simplify that difficult technique (so elusively un-attainable) of recognising 'patination' on silver. His comments on the 'amateur-fringe' of so-called 'antique dealers' will be much appreciated by all hard-working honest men and women whose lives, finances and dreams revolve around their profession. For, although antique dealers are deemed to be mere 'traders', theirs is a vocation which cannot but be termed 'profession'. It is always pleasant to peruse the considered work of a true professional.

Eric Delieb.

Preface

This book is my attempt to help the inexperienced collector avoid numerous costly mistakes—to be 'done rotten' is a variant phrase that I have heard in the street markets—before he acquires discretion and discernment.

My interest in and affection for fine antique silver extends over thirty years. Although there have been several long periods of inactivity in its pursuit and study, I *do* reckon that I have spent at least a decade of everyday handling and thinking about silver in the normal course of business. I have little doubt that the majority of my readers would have obtained a commensurable knowledge in half the time that it took me.

It is my intention to put all collectors on their guard, to protect them against the numerous dangers in the 'jungle'—these I will describe in detail—and put them on a path which, if pursued intelligently and resolutely, will lead them in six months instead of thirty years to a sound working knowledge of our subject. The course should be acceptable principally for beginners and also to those numerous dealers and auctioneers of absolute integrity but less experience who wish to take a justifiable pride in their stock and/or conduct of business.

I do not believe that a book of this type has been attempted before and I suggest some reasons for this:

1. It will hurt the feelings of many inexperienced collectors because they may resent my (or anyone else's) inference that their collection, up to the present, is not the best in the world. If, after reading this book, they care to inspect their collection in the light of their increased knowledge and decide that I'm absolutely right,

and agree that they have been led astray, they might possibly be so piquéd as to give up collecting altogether.

2. Certain sections of the trade may, without any legitimate reason, regard this work as damaging to business.

'What do you want to tell 'em these secrets for? They'd never find 'em out if they collected all their lives,' said one dealer with friendly but sincere indignation, 'it's like trying to teach a child algebra before the alphabet.' Strangely enough I would trust the speaker implicitly in any transaction with his fellow traders, but his attitude, although typical of an influential minority of dealers, cannot be beneficial to the long-term interests of our business.

3. Finally, most authors, experts and professional journalists alike, who write books or articles in magazines on specialised subjects are too scholarly to stoop to the mundane practicality of this little book.

During my time in the silver trade I have got by fairly successfully without acquiring as yet any real knowledge of the processes of construction employed by the old-time craftsmen, and so I will not touch upon this side of our subject. I have also avoided involvement in overly technical aspects. A good knowledge of styles for periods, the immediate recognition of antique 'patination', careful inspection of articles and average common-sense are all that are required to decide with confidence if a piece under consideration is 'right', 'suspect' or 'wrong'.

Probably, captious critics may be irritated by the dogmatism and repetition of my warnings. In the same manner as a nail requires several blows before the point is secure, I do aver, although it is extremely rude of me, that 'dogmatism' and 'repetition' are necessary.

Even if the 'schedule of study' (chapter 14) is completed by only a minority of my readers, the rest of the work offers much information and assistance of a cautionary nature. If trainee collectors insist on buying silver before they are competent to do so, let them take this little book around with them. Chapter 15, in itself, entitled 'Routine Inspection of Silver' must surely serve them more reliably than any guide to hall-marks.

John Bateman Luddington.
Collectors' Corner,
Portobello Rd., W.11.

Acknowledgements

If I described the valuable and generous help that I have received in the writing of this book, I would embarrass those I wish to thank and bore my readers. Instead, I append a list of names that I shall always recall with gratitude.

Mr Eric Delieb.
Miss Judy Wentworth.
Mr R. P. T. Came and Messrs Sotheby.
Messrs Christie, Manson & Woods.
Mr J. W. Clark.
Mr Frank Elam.
Dr Michael Fordham.
Miss Lorraine Griffin of Messrs Sotheby.
Lady Anthony Hooper.
Maj. H. B. McCance.
Mr C. M. Maurice-Jones.
Miss Molly Pearce and Sheffield Museums.
Mr Philip Woolley.

The following gave me their kind permission and every facility either to borrow existing photographs or to take new ones.

Burroughs Wellcome Trust.
Messrs Christie, Manson & Woods.
Colchester Museum.
Major M. P. D. Cruickshank, M.C.

Dublin Museum.
The Rector and Churchwardens of Ilam Church, Northumber-
land.
Sheffield Museums.
Messrs Sotheby.
Messrs Tessier.
The Wine Label Circle.
The Worshipful Company of Goldsmiths.

Sketches by Miss Judy Wentworth on pages 96 and 106 to 109; by
Miss Victoria Seale (a 14-year-old pupil of St Paul's Girls' School) on
pages 25, 89 and 91.

I

How not to Collect

Behind the implications of this chapter lies the story of a wicked, wasted youth! Fortunately it is unnecessary to bore you with many details, but my sudden interest in silver was so disgracefully unplanned but rewarded by such fantastic good fortune, that some brief account of this *puerile muddle* must be worth any novice collectors' consideration if only to show them how not to go about things. Furthermore, if I can now claim to have as good a knowledge of our subject as most people, then you, ensuring that a repetition of the fortunate experiences that befell me are firmly in your grasp from the outset, should attain my standard of proficiency in a thirtieth of the time that it took me. Within a year of concentrated effort you can all surpass me easily, if, initially, you will stick diligently to the scheme of this course.

The cupidity and delight of collecting runs in my blood, inherited from my mother's family. Her two grandfathers were notable collectors. One, Thomas Bateman (d. 1861), the rather famous archaeologist and antiquarian, himself the son of a pioneer English archaeologist, Thomas Bateman senior, spent his entire life digging and searching; it is surprising that he retained sufficient energy to propagate. The other, Thomas Jessop, founder of Jessop Steel, at Sheffield, spent his life collecting all the money that accounted for the early deaths of most of his descendants after, but alas, not before they had accomplished a thorough job of dispersing both collections in dissolute pleasures!

Up to the age of five or six, I was an extremely keen archaeologist myself and might still be one today but for receiving a snub from which I have never recovered.

In the nursery with my governess, my reading of history had reached the reign of King Stephen, but all my playtime was spent digging for treasure in our garden at Ely. As a secondary interest, I was also hoping to discover a secret tunnel that was supposed to run under the garden in a direct line from Ely Cathedral to Little Downham church.

My discoveries, so far, would have been best described as of nursery rather than national importance and I was not unaware of a sense of failure.

My diggings had reached an area near the kitchen door of an untenanted house in the grounds and I was discovering an interesting variety of rusted kitchen implements, tins, broken cups and saucers and what looked like the skeleton of a cat when suddenly my spade unearthed a fabulous find! In a flash, I was aware that I had 'hit the bigtime', that the bottle in my slippery hands was of exceptional historical importance and of the twelfth century without a doubt!

Breathless with excitement, I rushed towards the house and stumbled up the stairs to the nursery, still clutching the trophy.

'Look!' I screamed, 'I've found the king's ink bottle, it says so on the label.' And indeed, printed in white lettering upon an ink-blue background were the exciting words: 'Stephen's Ink'!

After that, I graduated to birds' eggs and butterflies and moths without contributing much to the science of Natural History. Later, I gave up collecting altogether and instead, it was ponies and horses all the time: riding them, racing them and, finally, from the age of twenty-three, training them under both rules of racing until Hitler stopped it all.

Prudently thinking it was safer to hide in the clouds when battle commenced, I volunteered for flying training. I was told to report at a new Lincolnshire aerodrome where I was to work underground in the Operations Room until such time as there were sufficient aircraft to risk my tuition ... For the time being, I held the rank of aircraftsman, second class, and certainly held no desire to aspire higher in a Service for which I had neither aptitude nor experience.

In retrospect, I allow that the manner of my arrival at the aerodrome was unusual. I reported at the guardroom several days late and brought with me two racehorses and an apprentice jockey. I was confident of winning a race with one of the horses, 'Masseur' by name, if and when racing resumed and this, I hoped, would put all my misdemeanours right with the R.A.F. as obviously they were gambling men.

Having found stabling for the horses and lodgings for the apprentice, I then rushed round the local farms and rented all the available shooting in the locality. It was fortunate that I acted so promptly for I only just forestalled my Commanding Officer, bent on the same purpose.

Initially, I understand, the C.O. was a little 'put-out' on being informed by the farmers that he had lost the shooting to one of his airmen by a short head. Subsequently, he proved to be a splendid fellow and I arrived at a very agreeable understanding with him. Had it not been so, and had he had me posted away as an undesirable eccentric as, I believe, the Station Warrant Officer recommended, my activities in silver would have been still-born.

The C.O. gave me permission to work the racehorses round the perimeter of the landing-field without disturbing the game in the fields nearby, and all members of the Officers' Mess, and anyone who had a gun on the station, had a standing invitation to my shoots. During the 'phoney' war, we had a number of very pleasant parties with surprisingly few casualties either in game or service personnel.

Meanwhile, I had been installed in the Operations Room in charge of a very special 'watch' of W.A.A.F.S. They were supposed to have been picked for their intelligence, but I think there had been a slip-up for they seemed to have been chosen for their beauty by an officer of consummate good taste.... Discipline was very slack!

It was not long before most of these girls were donning Wellington boots and beating for us on the shoots. Some, accomplished horsewomen, rode the horses in their work.

'Masseur' won a race at Leicester and *even* the S.W.O. liked me then. But all good things come to an end. The game-shooting ended, racing finished, the serious shooting began and my wife arrived to keep an eye on me!

Thanks to 'Masseur', who was now out of the war and domiciled in Ireland, I had a bit of 'brass' to spare. Working in the Ops. Room, was a very nice Welsh poet called Theodore. Whilst supposedly on guard duty, he used to write odes to those few unfortunate birds that fell to our guns. Partly because my own sympathies lay a considerable way towards his, we became friends.

He advised me to invest my winnings in antique silver, which seemed to him to be ridiculously undervalued. I took his advice for want of something better to do.

The first shop I entered was situated on a steep hill in Lincoln; the medieval oak beams were scented by the smoke from centuries of log fires. An old man, with butterfly collar, black tie and pearl tie-pin advanced to greet me with a smile, and a manner as gracious as his shop. Without the slightest trepidation, I placed myself in his hands.

'I know nothing about silver,' I began, 'but I want to start collecting it. I was thinking of some small piece that I will never grow tired of. Will you help me, please?'

He thought for a moment and then pulled from a drawer a number of table spoons. He handled and inspected them all carefully before making his decision. 'This is your piece. It is a rat-tailed spoon of the Queen Anne period and bears the full set of Britannia Standard Chester Assay marks for the year 1712. It weighs 3 ozs 4 dwts and is of magnificent quality. The maker is...'

I could not wait to listen to further details. I had no idea that such magnificent spoons existed and, even today, I doubt if I have seen a better. I didn't enquire how much it was, but said: 'Thank you very much indeed. What do I owe you?'

What a fortunate shop to find at random! What a start!

Armed with this perfect piece as a model, and still without a guide to hall-marks, I toured through the Lincolnshire towns searching for further spoons. I bought a few, but as my standards were so fortuitously high from the outset, I already had some competence to reject the second-class. Unconsciously, too, because of the superb 'patina' on my first and subsequent spoons, I was already instinctively suspicious of spoons of a different colour. I had no reason for this suspicion: I had no idea that this different colour was probably caused by repaired shanks, re-shaped bowls or erased initials, but I did appreciate that they were unsuitable companions for my own spoons.

The next important step—also a fantastic stroke of luck—began while I was on leave in Northants. I entered a shop full of antiques of every description and asked an extremely dissipated-looking old dealer if he had any silver. He told me he had a Victorian coffee pot and because he placed it in my hands before I had time to say I wasn't interested in Victoriana, I felt compelled to examine it. It had the same soft colour and simple lines as my spoons. On the lid was a strange finial that opened and shut on a hinge. The marks seemed to me to be London, Britannia Standard period, like most of my spoons!

'Isn't it early eighteenth century?' I enquired.

'No, no, my boy. It's Dublin, Victorian.'

'Well, anyhow, I like it,' I replied, only half convinced by my correction, 'how much is it?'

'Eleven pounds to you, my boy.'

I was inclined to ask how much it would have been to anyone else, but respect for such a venerable dissipation restrained me. I paid up and departed.

Immediately I got home, I consulted my recently acquired guide to hall-marks, compiled by the late Mr F. Bradbury of Sheffield, and confirmed that the date was London, 1719. On opening 'Jackson's', a recent gift to me, I discovered that the maker was Augustin Court-auld. A picture in my scrap-book of illustrations and descriptions of silver indicated that the 'coffee' pot was actually a chocolate pot. This explained the hinged finial that would allow some slender instrument to be inserted to stir the chocolate. It seemed possible that I had obtained an interesting piece for a modest outlay.

Some days later, I had an introduction to visit Mr Frederick Bradbury, the well-known authority on Sheffield Plate and antique silver. He was a charming old man and only too pleased to help a poor chap in the R.A.F. He showed me his collections and then I showed him my chocolate pot. 'What a pity,' he said, 'that the coat of arms engraved on this applied shield is of a slightly later date. The shield probably conceals the original coat underneath and it shouldn't be there. We'll have to get it off for you. It will spoil the "patina", of course, but it will be more valuable without the shield.'

I didn't know what 'patina' meant (although I already recognised it) and forgot or was too ashamed of my ignorance to ask. I accepted Mr Bradbury's advice without question.

In retrospect, at a much later date, I believe the removal of the applied shield was unjustified. The substituted coat, as Mr Bradbury had told me, was only of slightly later date. I think he wanted to have a look at the original coat underneath.

When the pot arrived back, I was dismayed. I could scarcely bear to look at it. A few days before, I had owned an object of beauty and now even its simple, graceful lines were forgotten under the garish shimmer of high polish.

But even this misfortune proved as valuable an experience as any beginner could have had.

In disgust, and without bothering to ascertain its value, I advertised to sell the offending piece in *The Times*: 'chocolate pot, London 1719 by Augustin Courtauld. £30'. During lunch on the same day as the advertisement appeared, an enormous car pulled up at the door. A dealer from London, 150 miles away, had arrived to buy. The alacrity of this powerful car's arrival, when petrol was so strictly rationed, suggested to me that I had undervalued my pot. Besides, I took an instinctive dislike to this dealer. I fobbed him off and then sent the pot to auction where it fetched £80.

I suppose a chocolate pot of 1719 would have fetched £200 in those far off days, if in good condition, and so, considering that the 'patina' of my pot was completely ruined and that the traces of the original coat were unsightly, the figure of £80 checks quite reasonably with our conclusions in chapter 12 (b).

Realising now that even 'ruined' silver was worth money, my standards dropped for a considerable time and, instead of collecting fine specimens, I began searching for bargains. I did not enjoy myself as much, and I was insufficiently experienced to avoid 'burning my fingers'. But my early experiences had shown me what I required for my personal collection and this is why I was a very lucky man. I still sometimes recall the aroma of those oak beams in Lincoln when I spot a piece of outstanding quality.

2

An Abridged Survey of Your Dangers

When someone comes to write a history of the nineteen sixties it
will be incomplete without mention of the British public's extra-
ordinary craze for collecting 'trivia', which developed in this
decade. So-called 'antique' markets and new shops, stocking the
mostly tasteless products of the late nineteenth and early twentieth
centuries (and later!) have sprung up like 'mushrooms' throughout
London and the provinces, and now it seems almost as if half the
population is engaged in selling 'antiques'! People of my generation
tend to feel a little hurt when they see our erstwhile playthings sold
as antique! These new dealers may know almost as little about
antiques as many of their customers.

But for the fact that everyone—sellers, buyers and the manufacturers of 'antiques'—seems to be enjoying themselves enormously,
one would assume that the strains and stresses of modern life had
shattered the nation's reason. Nevertheless, one cannot believe that
the public is making wise investments.

As supplies of pewter, wood-carvings, small pieces of furniture,
'Mary Gregory' glass, pot-lids, Cranberry ware, silver caddy spoons
and suchlike become exhausted or expensive, the 'wide boys' in
their back street workshops began and continue to meet the public's
demand.

Because of the heavy penalties to be risked, mass forgeries of silver
articles are rare; but someone has conceived the idea of buying up as
many worn-out late Georgian tea spoons as he could lay his hands on
and turning them into caddy spoons. He removes a section of the

stem, leaving the hall-marks untouched, and then joins the stem together again; the worn-out bowl is reshaped and embossed with fruit and leafage and the whole new spoon is then gilt to conceal the join on the stem. A few months ago, these forgeries were everywhere. Legislation has subsequently stopped this anomaly.

In about 1963, the public began to turn its attention to silver. Many countries in the world have provided a ready market for English silver over many years, but apart from a hard core of collectors and a few shrewd businessmen with an eye for a sound investment, only since 1963 has it received belated recognition. Prices in the London and provincial auction rooms began to soar; the public read all about it in the press and decided to 'have a go'.

Antique silver at this time was ridiculously under-priced and the uninterrupted rise in prices that *top quality* silver has experienced ever since—even throughout the current economic 'squeeze'—was caused, I fear, not because purchasers loved old silver, but because they deemed it, with its world-wide appeal, as a 'gilt-edged' hedge against inflation.

The investors at that time, as they still are today, were chiefly big dealers, the 'lions' of business, and stockbrokers. The latter groups, being shrewd enough to appreciate the risks of trying to invest in a commodity about which they knew practically nothing, commissioned dealers to select and buy for them. I have no doubt that these business tycoons made a full investigation into both the integrity and the experience of their selected dealer. They behaved very sensibly and dealers thoroughly enjoy building up a client's collection with top quality silver which we are confident will appreciate in value most handsomely as the years progress. My only sorrow is that so many investors regard their purchases purely as commercial objectives and may 'miss-out' on the pleasures that such works of art, craftsmanship and interest should afford them.

But the poor old members of the general public, who tried to invest in silver with little available capital, started off and usually continued out of step. Perhaps, they think, quite erroneously, that the long-established dealers do not want to be bothered with them.

Instead of putting themselves in reliable hands and making an occasional small but worth-while investment, they tend to fritter their money away on flimsy, mass-produced, silver knick-knacks often devoid of any merit whatsoever. At best, or maybe at worst, they purchase what was once a genuine Georgian article long since worn out—a spoon for example—with the bowl re-shaped, embossed (like the caddy spoons mentioned earlier) within the last few months or years in a crude design of fruits and leafage and called in the trade a 'berry spoon'. The original Georgian hall-marks are still visible and so, thinks the customer, 'it is a genuine antique'. Tourists from overseas are also 'suckers' for this type of ornate nonsense.

FIGURE *1*. *A mid-eighteenth century tankard embossed in the second half of the nineteenth century and therefore unrepresentative of either period. It is necessary and interesting to record that although the young artist was asked to reproduce all the ponderous detail of Victorian decoration, she decided for her own aesthetic satisfaction to modify and improve upon it and thus she sketched quite a pleasing design, flattering but still similar to the nineteenth century taste.*

In the numerous antique markets, both outdoor and indoor, there are very many absolutely honest dealers, but there is only a sprinkling of expertise and it is in such places that the experienced eye can very occasionally spot an interesting bargain. They are light-hearted, friendly places and well worth your visits. But the inexperienced collector would be chancing his luck much too far if he attempted at the outset to buy antique silver from 'immature' dealers. The same warning must apply to many shops all over the country unless they be long-established specialists.

As one walks through the markets, one often encounters little groups of dealers and customers, all trying to help each other, as they peer backwards and forwards between their guide to English hall-marks and, for example, a late nineteenth century continental article. 'It's London, 1710' one suggests with enthusiasm, whilst another, more gloomy, suggests 'Birmingham, 1925'.

Unless purchased from a reputable authority, I cannot emphasise too strongly that it is highly dangerous for anyone, dealer or collector, to purchase any item if they still feel the need of a guide to hall-marks before they can recognise, almost at first glance, the origin and approximate date of any silver item.

Except perhaps at Christie's or Sotheby's (as I will explain later) it is just as dangerous for the inexperienced to buy at auctions as in shops and markets. It is at auctions that many dealers get rid of their sub-standard stock.

Recently, a woman stallholder in the Portobello road came to me with a tablespoon by Hester Bateman. She wanted six pounds for it. The marks were satisfactory, but I have never seen a spoon with a bowl so startling. In shape and quality it resembled a flying saucer suffering from metal fatigue and in imminent danger of complete disintegration.

'Oh, no!' I said, 'I can't hold myself responsible for this thing.' 'Nor can I,' she replied. Thus, there was an understanding between us and I thought of a way to help her.

'I'm selling some junk at auction in the country this Thursday,' I said, 'and I'll get them to take this spoon for you. There are a lot of new dealers down there and they'll buy anything by Hester. I'm certain it will fetch seven or eight pounds.'

My new friend hesitated and I decided that she needed spot cash. I elected to buy it and sell it at the auction myself. The spoon fetched fifteen pounds ten shillings; bought by the daughter of a well-known local family, who had just commenced the fashionable game of 'antique-dealing'.

'One fool will usually find another in a country auction room,' said one dealer to whom I told the story, 'or was it you or the auctioneer "running her up"?' 'We would have been even bigger fools if we'd taken such a risk,' I replied.

There may be fewer than one hundred real experts in antique English silver in the whole wide world and many of these are based in London. There are many dealers with brains like ready-reckoners and eyes like hawks who can assess the value and condition of the usual or popular items in a flash and with amazing accuracy, but they may be out-of-their-depth when confronted by the unusual.

Mr X is one of the biggest and most popular dealers in the world and the bulk of his stock is of superb quality. Unfortunately, because of his very considerable interests overseas, where collectors are generally even less particular than in London, he deals also in second and third quality goods. He has been buying and selling enormous quantities of silver every day for about fifty years. He 'thinks silver' all day long and probably dreams of it. Nevertheless, I would hesitate to consider Mr X as among the leading hundred experts in the world.

I happened to be dining with Mr X in a provincial hotel. 'I suppose, by now,' I said, 'you must know everything there is to know about silver.' Mr X did not even pause to think: 'Good God, no! I pick up something new every week.' Later that same evening, Mr X told me a curious tale, that worries me still as I try to follow the processes of his mind.

'I had a good customer who wanted a James II lidded tankard,' Mr X began, 'and all I had in stock was one which the Victorians had embossed and which I had had beaten out flat again for overseas. I could have let this go for a thousand, but I reckoned that my customer would think that too cheap, and would be worried there was something wrong with it. He was an old customer and I wanted him satisfied so I charged him two thousand. Some months later, he came back rather cross to return it because some friend of his had told him that it had been dechased. He even started lecturing me about hammer marks and then found a complete, bloody Bachanalian grape against the rim that had got missed out.'

'You try and do your best for customers,' Mr X added in a pained voice 'and that's all the thanks you get ...'

3

False Confidence

Mr X's modest admission that even after fifty years he was still learning about silver led to an amusing sequel a few weeks later. I was trying to explain some point of interest about an early spoon to a youth in his late 'teens. 'As a matter of fact, I happen to know all about silver,' he said. 'How very interesting! and may I ask you where you work?' 'I'm with Mr X.'

I pursued the matter no further, but I might have replied: 'In your present frame of mind it may still be several years before you are fit to do anything but clean Mr X's silver.'

But we should excuse the boy's unwarranted confidence. I went through the same silly stage of 'knowing it all' in about 1945-1947 and I believe that almost all collectors experience the same infantile and often very painful teething troubles.

It is only when we are fully aware of the abysmal depths of our ignorance that we begin to understand the wide scope of our subject and really start to learn. All this is odd because in our first year we are humble and diffident enough; then something awful happens. Perhaps we are overwhelmed with glee in picking up an exciting bargain from someone many years our senior in experience. We are in danger as great as the boy who is unlucky enough to enjoy a large win on the horses with his first bet!

Up to the late spring of 1969, before the 'squeeze' really began to 'bite', when prices of all qualities of silver seemed to be rising by about 5% per week and had been so doing for a long period of time, a number of youths aged between fifteen and twenty-five tried to jump on the 'bandwagon'. At first they had no trade premises but bought and sold, or sold on commission to and for traders in the shops and markets, and accosted collectors searching for silver in the Portobello road.

Very soon they sported trade cards, some got premises in the West End of London, and having outgrown small, inexpensive pieces of silver, embarked on costly items, many of which were 'wrong'. Their arrogance and confidence became laughable and it was clear that they were riding for a heavy fall.

One of these young men told me that he was making over one thousand pounds a week, was taking offices in Bond Street and 'keeping a gorgeous bird' in an expensive London hotel.

Now, most of them have vanished leaving a trail of debts behind them.

Without trying to account for the antics of the mind (Freud might have been able to explain, I cannot), we can at least pin-point the cause of our unnecessarily long and painful apprenticeship: we have all started out down the deceptively innocent-looking paths of the 'silver jungle' unequipped and without a map. I hope this book will provide you with a reliable guide and necessary 'jungle' accoutrements.

4

Advice on What to Collect

In the course of my travels in pursuit of silver I have inspected innumerable stocks in shops and Antique Fairs throughout the country, and have also seen a number of private collections. I think it would be useful to present my observations in a statistical form. With this before our eyes, we can discuss it. I have not inspected many dealers' stocks overseas, but I have watched what the dealers from overseas buy in U.K.

	Av: Private Collection in U.K.	Av: Dealers' Stock in U.K.	Av: Dealers' Stock in N. America.	Av: Dealers' Stock in Europe.	Av: Stock in Top-Class Antique Fair or in Top-Class London Shop.
A. Forgeries:	5%	5%	8%	10%	0%
B. Altered Pieces:	15%	15%	22%	30%	5% (1)
C. Serious Repairs (visible):	5%	5%	0%	0%	5% (2)
D. Serious Repairs (hidden):	25%	25%	25%	25%	5%
E. Lesser Repairs or Second quality:	35%	35%	35%	30%	35%
F. Good Quality:	10%	10%	5%	5%	30%
G. Superb Quality:	5%	5%	5%	0%	20%

(1) A number of later-decorated pieces might be stocked.
(2) Exceptionally rare items in poor condition might be stocked.

Obviously, the amount of good quality antique silver remaining in this country is small and getting less each year. It does not take many years of everyday, rough use, to reduce silver from a superb state to a secondary condition, and museums from overseas can often outbid everyone when important items come on the market. Knowledgeable or well-advised private collectors from all corners of the earth usually by-pass their local retailers and buy direct from London.

It is certain that really good English silver is already in very short supply and the demand for it is keen.

During the current economic 'squeeze', we have seen 'run-of-the-mill' antique silver drop in value by some 40% but real collectors' gems, representing no more than 10% of all the silver in circulation, continue to harden by an approximate rate of 25% per annum.

All of us must surely have had some experience of collecting whether it be of postage stamps, butterflies or sea-shells. If, as a true collector, you had the free choice of 17½ indifferent shells or of one superb specimen, which would you choose?

Your answer reflects the precise reason why, according to a recent sales catalogue, a very poor George II pear-shaped cream jug was knocked down for £20 while a superb example of the same style and date obtained £350. And, moreover, if the economic 'squeeze' should continue with all its ferocity for another year it is quite likely that the poor jug would then be worth £12 while the fine jug might be worth between £400 and £500. However long you live, however important your collection may become, you will never tire of nor wish to sell an outstanding example of old silver, even if it be nothing more than a humble mid-Georgian tea spoon, which cost £4.

My confident advice to collectors and dealers is to collect the best, whatever it is and whenever you find it, either with good hallmarks, with maker's mark only or with no marks whatsoever, and don't worry too much about the cost because *the best is rare*.

Unless some article is required for everyday use, is of exceptional rarity, or has an important historical association, on no account purchase anything listed in the A, B, C and D categories of the statistical percentages in this chapter.

5

And Are There Bargains?

But for the general ignorance throughout the trade—and don't forget the fashionable 'dollies' playing at antique-dealing and sometimes affording their relatives a considerable disservice by selling their silver on commission—I very much doubt, if at this point in time, a specialist with a sense of responsibility to his customers could make a living; he must know more about his subject than his neighbours and be in a position to spot a bargain.

In the search for treasures 'no stone should be left unturned' but since none of us has either the necessary resolution or life-span to go to such extreme lengths, we must do the best we can. It must be remembered that every abortive expedition is one step nearer your next bargain. It is as foolish to be depressed by failure as to be unduly elated and made over-confident by success. If you keep on hunting you will be well rewarded every now and then and usually when you are least expecting it.

Many years ago I went to a country auction and arrived rather too early. Having inspected the silver on view, I glanced at my watch and noted that the village inn did not open for another ten minutes. To while away the time, I started fiddling with things—it irritates me when casual shoppers do the same with my stock—and happened to open the lid of one of those nineteenth-century, leather dressing cases. In those days there was no value attached to them beyond the silver content of the silver mounted and lidded glass containers, worth about fifteen shillings on average. From the recesses of the case my idle fingers removed a drawer and inside the drawer was a box that rattled. Amongst a quantity of hair-pins (and a thermometer which could have measured my sudden excitement) I saw a silver, six-inch ruler with a glorious 'patina'. A beautifully engraved inscription in Latin upon this unmarked treasure revealed that the ruler was donated by a royal tutor to a prince upon the occasion of the latter's birthday in 1639! After looking furtively over my shoulder to see that I was not observed I replaced the ruler, the box and the drawer and shut the lid of the case. I noted the lot (number 140) in my catalogue, but without checking the possibility of a printer's error, and then repaired to the nearby hostelry. Considering my excitement and the fact that I had made an early start with a long drive and without breakfast, it was an unwise move.

Some ninety minutes later I tore myself away from the inn with a belated recognition that time had flown and arrived back at the auction in a panic to hear the auctioneer calling 'lot 138'. I was not in a sufficiently composed state to cope with the problems that then beset me. Lot 140 was offered and was bought by me for fifteen shillings, but before I had had time to congratulate myself the auctioneer was offering another dressing case, exactly similar, unlisted in the catalogue and termed 'lot 140A'. Alas! very many of these large dressing-cases were to follow and I was obliged to buy all of them because of my uncertainty as to which one contained the ruler. By the time lot 140K had been sold the auctioneer was 'knocking' them down to me automatically and I, not so ugly in those far off days, and perhaps even a trifle effeminate in appearance, had become the 'butt' of all the wags in the tent.

I can't remember how many of those damned dressing-cases I bought, but I do recall that I was stopped by the police on my return journey for my car was both overloaded and without proper visibility. It was a very sobering experience, but my treasure afforded me great pleasure before it went the same way as most of the other interesting things that dealers buy....

Being now a rather grandfatherly figure and having a totally unwarranted reputation for being a kind man (with 'susceptible' I would have agreed), the local 'dollies' have, after losing a number of their relatives' treasures to me, got me 'taped'. Just as I am about to grab some interesting piece, they flicker their lovely, Jersey-cow-like eyes and say: 'Please, John, will you tell me a fair price to ask for that?'

Alas! no more bargains for me from this quarter.

In one respect, the private collector has an advantage over a dealer. There are a number of provincial dealers, usually sour, middle-aged spinsters, who refuse to part with anything if they suspect one is 'trade'. Knowing little or nothing themselves, they work on the principle that 'if it's worth that to him it's probably worth more to me'. Probably, they're right! And yet, on the other hand, many provincial dealers of this type are 'inverted snobs' who prefer to sell cheaply to a so-called 'collector'—who then boasts all over town of the ignorance of the country dealer—than sell at a fair price to a dealer, who would return regularly for more interesting articles. In these circumstances, such dealers are remarkably short-sighted.

The experienced collector can enter the most expensive shops and somewhere amongst the stock he is likely to find the odd something considerably below its market value: everyone slips up occasionally.

The provincial shop with its expertise (if any) specialised in furniture or porcelain, but carrying a fair stock of silver, is a highly promising covert to draw, especially if you're in time to catch the proprietor when he's just back from a private 'buy'.

There is an occasional bargain, usually of a minor nature, to be picked up at the Bermondsey market on Fridays. Personally, I have never found anything worth buying before 8.30 a.m. which seems to discount the theory that you've got to be there at 6 a.m. I haven't been there for many months, but as I used to leave towards noon, I would sometimes see Eric Delieb, author of those splendid books *Investing in Silver* and *Silver Boxes*, just arriving. I have little doubt that he discovers rare treasures that everyone else misses!

Within the last few months in the Portobello Road on Saturdays, I have heard rumours of several 'kills'. I know that a pair of Batswing wine labels, maybe worth £350, were bought for a small sum but I did not see them. I myself bought an unmarked Scottish quaich, circa 1800 and worth about £40, for 30/–. Far more exciting was the unmarked, late Elizabethan toilet box which a 'runner' brought me and *allowed* me to buy for £15! If it is a toilet box, it must be the only one of this early period so far discovered but it is difficult to give a firm ascription to an item that no one has seen before.

The story behind this bargain is interesting. A big dealer 'chucked' this unmarked box out of his shop virtually for nothing. Subsequently, it changed hands at £6. 10. and was then displayed on an outside stall in the Portobello Road, with 'the world and his wife' passing by, for two Saturdays before it was brought to me in Collectors' Corner at tea-time. Confronted by the unknown, certain only of its period and before I had had time to think, I nearly passed it on for £250 within two minutes of buying it.

I hope that my contentment with the beauty of my toilet box during a particularly difficult period of my life, is some compensation to the several dealers and 'runners' who handled it and might so easily have recognised it before I. The engraved decoration on the circular lidded box with its blue-tinted 'patina' in restful contrast to the quaintly engraved hunting scenes 'popping' in and out of arabesques, is quite similar to that on the rims on the set of six plates (London hall-marks for 1573-4) on view at the Victoria and Albert Museum.

Thrilled as I was, and will always be, with this little treasure, I was by no means satisfied with the knob in the centre of the tightly fitting lid and which facilitated its removal and replacement. The inevitable contrast between the two excellent 'patinations'—whiter on the solid knop than on the comparatively thin silver forming the body and lid—seemed far more pronounced than I expected and so I took it along to a museum, well experienced with Elizabethan silver, for a better opinion.

As I sat in a waiting-room, after surrendering the box for inspection, I heard little 'ahs', 'ohs' and cooings coming from the experts and assistants as they were summoned from various rooms so as not to miss seeing a piece so interesting. With 'ears on stalks', but unable to watch round a half-closed door, there was little doubt that they were examining my box and because I had fallen in love with it I glowed with pleasure to realise that others were enraptured too.

Eventually the murmurings subsided and an official emerged. 'We are inclined to agree with your ascription and we also think that the knop is a contemporary one,' he said, 'but we would like our expert on Eastern Silver to see it. I wonder if you would kindly leave the box with us until tomorrow afternoon?'

As I walked away without my treasure I was weighed down by misgivings. I could not seriously accept an expert's implication that the box might be of oriental origin, and I believed that a tactful excuse had been schemed for its retention! Either the museum was thinking of buying it, and required time to consult another expert, or my box was on a list of stolen items and I was a suspected 'fence'! Certainly the official's charming manner had not suggested the embarrassing possibilities of the latter situation, but the charm could have been an act designed to lull my suspicions and ensure my return for questioning by the police. After all, I had only known the runner who had sold the box to me for a few months.

The twenty-four hour period before collecting the box was quite miserable. When I presented myself once again at the museum I was immediately led towards an inner sanctum. *En route* there, I glanced at the foot-wear of every one I passed and I did not recover my equanimity until I had been informed by the expert that the museum was interested in buying the box and we were both laughing about my erstwhile fears. I promised to give the museum first refusal of the toilet-box if I did decide to relinquish it so soon and I expressed my sorrow that I could not afford to present it. But one day I hope it will grace a case in a museum. There it will be enjoyed by everyone who loves old silver.

Charity shops, bazaars and 'white elephant' stalls still produce occasional bargains even though local dealers, in the hope of getting a first picking of the goods donated for sale, vie with each other to get on the list of 'voluntary helps'—I know one or two who have even become 'pillars of respectability' to further their objectives. Recently, I have seen a good Queen Anne snuff-box which cost £5 and a George III cake basket which was sold as plate at a Red Cross sale for 10/–. Then there is the authentic story of the collector who bought a single George III candlestick in a charity shop for £10. As the assistant was wrapping it up, she added a pertinent afterthought: 'We've got another three of them in the back.' This collector, at least, had the decency to send a handsome donation to the charity concerned.

But, please! never forget that any very beautiful or interesting piece of antique silver, if in exceptionally fine condition, is always a bargain. Don't be too price conscious.

6

Hall-Marks are a Fool's Paradise

Many readers will be incredulous when I assert that the greater part of the most important examples of English silver are totally unmarked. At any important exhibition of English Medieval Art in silver, one would not expect to see more than 40 per cent of the exhibits with any marks whatsoever.

There are several reasons which I will suggest, why so much important plate went unmarked, even occasionally into the early part of the nineteenth century, but I will not touch upon the numerous statutes relating to hall-marks which commenced in 1300, and which are explained in full detail by the late Sir Charles Jackson in his monumental *English Goldsmiths and Their Marks*. This, of course, is a book that all must use.

There is evidence to suggest that by the sixteenth century the nobility and gentry preferred to purchase silver with London hallmarks, but this, I think, was only because the London craftsmen enjoyed a reputation for a quality of work superior to that of their provincial rivals. If, on the other hand, the provincial customer had the confidence to bestow his patronage in support of a local silversmith, then the desirability of marks did not arise. Indeed, if the patron was in a hurry for his orders, he would not have wished them subjected to the inevitable two-way delays between silversmith and assay office when administration and despatch were possibly but little faster than the postal and official services in 1970!

All this apparent flouting of the statutes relating to hall-marks seems to have been due to a gentlemen's agreement between the local assay authorities and the London and provincial silversmiths, whereby the former agreed to turn a blind eye upon all silver executed for private orders.

This theory is supported by circumstantial evidence alone because whereas almost all the 'bread and butter' goods of early periods, such as spoons, drinking vessels, Ecclesiastical Plate, etc, made and retailed in considerable quantities, were fully marked, many of the more unusual pieces were left unmarked.

As it is not requisite to mark silver ordered for the royal household, and because it is unlikely that silversmiths making something rather extra special for their own household would bother to get this work assayed, it is understandable that these unmarked pieces are often of exceptional quality.

Following the slightly fussy 'tulip and acanthus' motif enrichment of the Post-Restoration period and the somewhat cumbersome styles, initially, of the Huguenot refugees at the end of the century (Pierre Harache, for whom Simon Gribelin worked as an engraver, was granted Freedom by Redemption of the London Goldsmiths' Company in 1682), the popular taste turned to simplicity of design in the early years of the eighteenth century. There are indications that some craftsmen bitterly resented the compulsory intrusion of large, somewhat bellicose-looking Britannia Standard marks biting savagely into their magnificent work. Where practicable, hall-marks were usually positioned concealed from the eye.

If an article consisted of several parts, such as a Queen Anne oil and vinegar cruet, with its two silver bottle-tops and very small castor, it was not unusual for the set to be assayed as one unit on the underneath of the footed cruet-stand with the total weight of all silver parts comprising the set scratched nearby. I have seen only two complete specimens of this type and period of cruet but both were marked in the manner described. In the course of time most of these early cruet frames have disappeared but a number of their fine, small castors (very possibly used originally for ginger) survive.

It could be argued that such unmarked pieces might have been made for special orders at a considerably later date to replace those damaged or stolen but it is unlikely that replacement castors (unless made within a few years of the originals) would either conform precisely with the style of the original period or bear a replica of the original Coat-of-Arms or other device. Finally, of course, there is the appearance of the 'patina' to consider, for this will indicate an approximate age. A combination of these three 'witnesses' would take me far less time to examine for authenticity than a piece with indifferent 'patination' but with full hall-marks.

It interests me to think, too, that some of the unmarked pieces that we find, sometimes costing us a ridiculously low figure, were originally captured by highwaymen when a consignment was *en route* to an assay-office.

There is no denying the fact that a bold set of hall-marks accompanied by the mark of a famous maker is a very satisfying 'extra' on a fine piece of antique silver. But in my case, I fear, this satisfaction is kindled by cupidity, due to the marketable, additional interest that good marks convey to the majority, and certainly not from any aesthetic consideration.

Nothing written in this section should deter collectors from seeking and appreciating rare sets of marks for this is an enthralling sideline of collecting that sometimes helps us all with research and leads to a better understanding of our subject. What I have written is designed to put hall-marks in a suitable perspective so that collectors may appreciate the quality of an item in preference to its rather ugly marks.

The commercial reaction to unmarked items of fine quality in the big London auction rooms is changing. A perfect unmarked item, virtually identical to a fully-marked piece of equal quality, might now obtain almost half the price of the latter. Ten years ago, it would have fetched less than one quarter of the price. The same unmarked piece, today, would realise very much more than a similar fully-marked item of indifferent quality.

If our subject grows generally better understood, the same tendency towards a more enlightened appreciation of unmarked pieces should continue.

Obviously, silver hall-marks are not stamped on any other types of antiques, but the experts in these other fields do not worry. They, as you should do with silver, have taken the trouble to learn their subject and to profit by the ignorance of the majority!

This is the age of 'instant' things, and some would wish to attain their knowledge of antiques as quickly as a cup of coffee, but they who in five minutes learn how to identify hall-marks from a pocketguide are in greater danger than those in the position of knowing nothing at all.

It was one of these pocket-guides that caused the expulsion of a woman dealer from one of the London antique markets for consistently selling modern silver as Georgian. This was a little unjust, I think, for surely she was a fool rather than a rogue. Passing her stall, I heard a heated argument in progress. She tried to enlist my aid: 'This customer says this basket isn't Georgian silver—look,' and she pointed triumphantly to a London date cycle in her pocket guide, 'I knew I was right! It's London, 1950—George the sixth.'

7

Marks: Forged and Otherwise

The Wardens of Goldsmiths' Hall have, by reason of a number of charters granted to them since 1327, wide powers to control the Goldsmiths' and Silversmiths' craft. These powers represent such a power in our modern state that although still exercising their right to search for, seize and destroy spurious plate, they can punish offenders. When they consider that a prosecution is necessary, suspects are passed to the comparative clemency of our legal system.

It must be some time since the Wardens have deported, imprisoned, or placed offenders in the pillory after slicing off both ears. On the debit side, we are confronted by the increase of the falsification of antique plate. In modern history the two most notorious periods for such activities are in the second half of the last century and today.

I encountered the powers of Goldsmiths' Hall many years ago, I was buried away in the country, soon after I had started dealing in silver. There was a knock on my door and a Mr Lindsey, the then Deputy Warden, announced his desire to inspect my stock. With a conscience as clear as crystal, I made him welcome and with the naïve confidence of most inexperienced dealers showed him my silver with pride and pleasure. Everything went well until he spotted a Queen Anne chamber candlestick—the very item for which, subsequently I was sure, he had expressly made the long journey from London to view—which I had bought at a big London auction earlier in the week at a price so cheap that an experienced dealer would have 'smelled a rat' immediately.

Unfortunately I have forgotten all details as to why this piece was a suspected forgery. Mr Lindsey took it away, leaving me unencumbered by the pillory, still in possession of my ears and with a kind, much valued invitation to visit him and be shown round Goldsmiths' Hall. He could only state that the chamberstick would be examined by the 'Antique Plate Committee' at their next monthly sitting in Goldsmiths' Hall and that I would then be informed of its findings.

After the piece had been condemned by the committee and destroyed, and I had been reimbursed by the auctioneers who sold it, it would seem that I was left in credit from this incident by an instructive tour of Goldsmiths' Hall and a greater awareness of the dangers and responsibilities of a reputable dealer. Actually, I was upset.

I had reasonable grounds—but I forget what they were—for believing, rightly or wrongly, that a very prominent dealer had alerted Mr Lindsey about this chamberstick and sent him in hot pursuit. In my inexperience, I attributed unworthy motives for this suspected action by the dealer. Today, I appreciate that it is the duty of experienced collectors and dealers, wherever practicable, to assist Goldsmiths' Hall to seize all spurious plate they see around. Obviously, too, all dealers and collectors should, whenever possible, co-operate with the Police when they suspect they are being offered stolen property.

It is the fear of unpopularity and the subsequent possible loss of business or bargains that deters so many of us from doing our duty.

We cannot expect the officials of the Goldsmiths' Company to conduct routine inspections of the stocks of dealers throughout the British Isles. To do such a job thoroughly would require the full-time employment of at least six experts in the London area alone.

Fortunately almost all forgers, past and present, seem totally ignorant of our subject and their efforts are almost invariably, except with early spoons, unrepresentative of even an approximate period and style; so forgeries can be likened to hybrids. Even when the forger chooses to superimpose a full set of marks, possibly cut from a Stuart piece, on the base of a genuine, unmarked tankard, the odds are about fifty to one on the forger selecting the wrong set of marks for the period.

Forgers display the same ignorance when putting a complete set of hall-marks from one object into another as when they forge their own sets of marks and strike such punches on unmarked or re-fashioned pieces. In the former case if you breathe on the hall-marks the insertion lines will normally become clearly visible. I have en-countered antique hall-marks inserted into modern pieces and I have also found such items plated in an attempt to conceal the insertion lines. Very recently I saw a pair of embossed Edwardian flower vases that had been soldered at the bottoms to the erstwhile bases of a pair of worn-out, circular salt cellars, still boasting a clear set of George III marks!

I am convinced that the greatest compliment an expert is likely to pay, unconsciously and *very* occasionally, to these types of for-geries is to reject them instantly and irrevocably without bothering to inspect the marks, thereby indicating no immediate recognition of fraud, but just an instinctive distaste for, and lack of interest in, antique silver that is so clearly below his desired standards.

Forged spoons of the sixteenth and seventeenth centuries have been cast from genuine spoons in considerable quantities. They are easy to recognise because of the 'woolliness' or lack of sharpness of the marks. Most of these forgeries are confined to Seal Top and Apostle spoons, the two most popular types, and purport to be Lon-don spoons. I have heard of a number of provincial spoons with early, forged marks and these frauds are harder to detect owing to the poorness of the workmanship.

Far more dangerous than the cast spoons are some very fine for-geries perpetrated, I suppose, towards the end of the last century. A talented rascal made excellent punch-marks in close imitation of the small sized punches used by the London Assay Office on the slender shanks of seal top spoons, which, when struck deep into the shanks and bowls, are extremely difficult to compare in detail with the genuine. I have handled such a spurious spoon and but for the curious lateness and uncertainty of the date-letter, which appeared to represent London 1673, on a spoon that I considered to be circa 1640, I am certain that I would have been fooled. The Victoria and Albert Museum considered this spoon to be the best forgery that they had ever seen, but this was no more than an opinion, and I handed it back to the owner with the recommendation that he should place it before the 'Antique Plate Committee' for a ruling. Before this could be done, the suspected forgery was stolen by burglars and I wonder if the owner claimed compensation from his insurers.

On another occasion, while waiting at the metalwork department of the 'V & A', a man seeking expert opinion came in with three seal top spoons. He thought one of them might be 'wrong', but that the other two should be 'right' because he had bought them at a big London auction. From a very cursory glance, which I hope went unnoticed, they all looked 'probables' to me, but the 'V & A' opined that all three were spurious. I was unable to hear the explanations.

Extreme precautions are necessary when purchasing spoons of the first half of the seventeenth century and earlier.

Spurious makers' marks would be virtually pointless unless the marks of very famous makers such as Paul de Lamerie, Paul Storr or Hester Bateman are concerned. But the styles of all three silversmiths mentioned are so distinctive, and the quality of the work of the first two so exceptional, that an intelligent forger would find it almost impossible to obtain suitable silver upon which to stamp his spurious mark.

For some time I have heard rumours of someone punching a forged Hester Bateman mark and at last I have seen an example of it. I noticed it at a small London auction upon a clumsily designed caddy spoon, genuinely assayed at London and within Hester's period. Although the maker's mark was a clever imitation—even although it seemed to 'quake'—of the mark she registered on August the third, 1787, few people could have thought that such an ugly piece emanated from Hester's factory. It was sold for very little more than it would have obtained without a maker's mark. Since beginning this book, I have seen another example of this spurious mark upon a set of coffee spoons. It seems that this forger must be active.

The gains to be made by such activity are attractive and the collector should always inspect makers' marks with the greatest care.

Quite frequently we find Georgian silver, usually circa 1800, with one maker's mark overstamping that of another. There is nothing sinister about this. In order to fulfil a rush order it was common practice for one silversmith to buy from another and punch his own mark upon his purchase before delivery to the customer. Many items of silver made by Hester Bateman were overstruck by another maker with the initials 'G.G.' (We believe these initials represent the maker's marks of either George Giles or George Gray, both London silversmiths). Between 1842-1867, a diamond-shaped mark is occasionally found on English silver in addition to the normal hallmarks. This is called a 'Registry of Designs Mark'. A full list of the 'registry marks' is given on pages 225/226 of Patricia Wardle's *Victorian Silver and Silver-plate* (Herbert Jenkins, 1963).

Wherever there was a considerable number of prosperous British emigrants we find silversmiths, often emigrants themselves, who catered for them. Thus, silver was made in the late Georgian period in Calcutta, Canton, the West Indies and Bermuda, and even earlier, in Canada and South Africa. In the middle of the nineteenth century much silver was wrought in Australia. Presumably in order to make their customers feel at home many of the local silversmiths made crude imitations of the London and provincial hall-marks and punched them on their wares. In style, these craftsmen tended to conform, more or less, with those in vogue within the mother country. Because there are avid collectors for silver made at Cape Town and in Canada and Australia, these Colonial products, of otherwise no exceptional merit, are much sought after and prices are high. If the marks on a piece of genuine-looking antique plate are so crude as to do injustice even to a local forger, they are likely to be of Colonial origin. Many small dealers are both ignorant and suspicious of Colonial marked pieces and sometimes they can be acquired very cheaply indeed.

It is not within the scope of this book to discuss Colonial silver in considerable detail. The imitation English marks (Viz: a lion passant, king's head, anchor or crown) punched on many Colonial pieces are regarded as spurious in this country, but they can be valuable forgeries and, if antique (i.e. at least one hundred years old), are tolerated by the Goldsmiths' Company and are therefore not impounded. Auctioneers and dealers infringe the current regulations only when selling Colonial silver that does not qualify as antique; but items wrought in the Colonies just before or after the turn of the last century are often considered to be antique by less experienced traders and are sometimes sold as such in error. Collectors are advised to tread warily.

Maybe, at some future date, the Goldsmiths' Company will reverse their ruling about later Colonial plate and this would please many people. But can our historical institutions afford to squander traditions and standards, which, although seeming to incense some sections of the community, have undoubtedly helped to earn this old country the grudging respect and confidence of much of the world? If all Colonial silver (and some of it is of sub-standard quality) was allowed to circulate freely in this country, the 'wide boys' would enjoy greater scope and have little difficulty in imitating the crude English hall-marks so often punched thereon.

At this stage it is understandable if my readers feel that the complexities and dangers of forged hall-marks are more than they will ever be able to cope with. This is a healthy frame of mind and assists in proving my point: that it is essential to become proficient both in the recognition of styles for periods and of antique 'patination' before the reader is competent to embark on purchases without expert advice. I will stress again that it is unwise to use a guide to hallmarks except to check the exact date of an item of silver after the collector has already established its approximate date.

By the time you have conscientiously completed the 'Schedule of Study' (chapter 14), you will certainly be at an advantage to the majority of dealers. If you will then adhere closely to the precautions described in chapter 15, the purchases you do make should, on balance, afford you constant pride and pleasure and should be an extremely sound financial investment. Already, hard though it may be to believe, even although the course outlined has scarcely begun, the reader is in some important respects better equipped to invest in silver than a majority of dealers and collectors.

In chapter 14 the problem of forged hall-marks will intrude again, but by this time they should appear in a much less menacing perspective.

Since completing this book, I have been reliably informed that a number of forgeries from Italy, mostly candlesticks and salvers in the mid-Georgian taste, are being smuggled into this country and hawked around the provincial shops by Italian travellers. I heard rumours of this intention about a year ago and endeavoured to alert the authorities. I have not seen any of these forgeries myself but understand that although the quality is extremely good the Italians are making mistakes with their spurious English hall-marks. Interpol, I am told, has been alerted.

8

Forgeries and Offending Pieces in General

The distinctions between forgeries and offending pieces are often academic, but conditions of silver listed under the latter and more charitable heading were frequently—especially in the last century—perpetrated in ignorance and without dishonest intent. The reader should refer to 'Jackson's' for detailed information of the regulations pertaining to hall-marks, but a useful précis of what does and what does not constitute a forgery, or an offending piece, can be contained in quite a few words.

Forgeries
   1. Any item with transposed, inserted or forged hall-marks.

Offending Pieces
   2. Any item that, subsequent to being marked, has been altered in form and purpose (viz: spoons into forks, teapots into tea caddies, pap boats into sauce or cream boats, tankards into jugs, etc). A piece which thus contravenes the regulations can be legalised with the co-operation of Goldsmiths' Hall by being restored to its original form and purpose, if possible, provided that all new pieces of silver used in the restoration are tested for sterling quality and, if acceptable, stamped with modern hall-marks.

This provides an explanation of, for example, a Charles II tankard bearing antique marks normally positioned, and a set of modern

47

marks where say, a Victorian-added lip has been removed and the resulting space filled up to restore its original form and purpose.

3. Any item that, subsequent to being marked, has received a substantial addition (viz: a rim to a salver): If the original marks are not tampered with, the piece can be legalised if the addition is assayed and struck with modern hall-marks.

Items Which Are Neither Forgeries Nor Offending Pieces

1. Items with non-contemporary decoration where the purposes of the article and the weight of the silver have not been changed by the alteration (viz: Georgian tankards and coffee pots, etc, with decoration inflicted in the Victorian era).

2. Items of silver which have been electro-plated in order to conceal unsightly repairs of a legitimate nature.

3. Marriages: where two or more parts, fully hall-marked but of different origins and either attached to each other or unattached, combine to make a complete article (and thus afford replacements for loss or damage).

Personally, I wish that items 1 and 2 under this heading were classified as offending pieces.

Note: No conditions of silver mentioned in this chapter, whether they be forgeries or not, must ever form part of my readers' collections.

9

Suggested Action When You See a Forgery

It is to be hoped that all readers will in due course co-operate in helping to reduce the number of forgeries and offending pieces in circulation.

The desirability of English silver overseas is very largely derived from the confidence instilled by our hall-marks and, apart from this national consideration, there is the worthwhile objective of trying to protect our own public and less experienced fellow collectors and dealers from dishonest 'wide-boys'.

Many inexperienced dealers, before they grow both fond and proud of our antique silver, tend to adopt an irresponsible attitude about forgeries and cannot understand why we are so concerned about them.

If, every time we spotted a forgery, we rang up Goldsmiths' Hall and reported the matter, our motives would be misunderstood and we might face bitter unpopularity.

Obviously, considerable tact is required in dealing with inexperienced dealers and collectors who are unwittingly in possession of forgeries. My own technique, which I am sure my readers can improve upon, runs along the following lines: I inspect the forgery and ask the dealer if any of his customers have commented upon it. Then, I ask him his own opinion of it and pretend to be most interested in every point he makes. Thus flattered, he is in a more receptive mood to listen to the points which I suggest. After this, he will invariably admit some doubts himself.

Having progressed this far, I ask him if he obtained a descriptive receipt when purchasing and if he considers there is any chance of his getting his money back. The reply to both these questions is usually in the negative because, most likely, it will have been bought from a 'runner'.

For a while, the dealer is complimented for his good taste as expressed in his stock, and nice things are said about the particularly discerning types of customers who are drawn to inspect his silver. We switch back to the forgery, and I point out what damage a suspect piece can do to a promising reputation. I suggest that it would be far the wisest thing for him to send the item for an opinion at Goldsmiths' Hall. I assure him that he will not have long to wait as the Antique Plate Committee meets monthly. I give him the address of Goldsmiths' Hall and receive his assurance that the piece will be sent.

Unfortunately, in order to keep faith with the dealer it is necessary to explain that in the event of his item being condemned he will not be permitted to have it back as it is. The Committee will recommend how it can be brought within the law if that is possible—for example, in the case of an altered piece it can sometimes be restored to its original condition. Alternatively, providing it is up to standard, it can be hallmarked as a new ware after erasure of the old marks. If it proved to be below the minimum standard however, it would have to be 'broken' and the dealer would then only recover the value of the silver content. The dealer would probably receive full compensation from the vendor if he had purchased the offending piece from a reputable source.

If the offending piece still remained in stock when I called next— but this has never happened—I would get in touch with Goldsmiths' Hall.

It is too much to hope that most of these forgeries that disappear from stock, as described, find their way to Goldsmiths' Hall and I do not pretend that I would attempt to adopt this technique with those dealers of a 'rougher' background, whom I am sure would merely reply with a torrent of abuse.

Certainly, the technique is nothing to be proud of; it is weak and devious and I hope that many of my readers will adopt a much stronger, more direct form of attack without upsetting nice people whose only sins, in this respect, are ignorance and wishful-thinking.

Nevertheless, my efforts do make dealers think about forgeries, do succeed in getting them removed from stock (even if they should appear again elsewhere!) and I am confident that, so far as his long-term business interests are concerned, they do the dealer a kindly action.

10

Learning to Recognise 'Patination'

Although concentrated effort of memory is necessary in the later stages of this course (chapter 14), by far the most difficult thing you have to do is described now.

When you can recognise a good, fair or poor patination—the excitement when you see a really good patina is full of compensation for all the effort expended—everything else becomes simple routine experience.

The beauty of antique silver is only 'skin deep'. When the finished article leaves the factory, it has a glittering, perhaps ostentatious polish without depth and without appeal to the enthusiast of antique silver. As the years go by, but without knowing anything of the scientific explanations—some say it is the result of the action of oxygen on the silver; others believe it is the gradual carbonisation of the alloys mixed with the silver; some say that it's all caused by gentle cleaning over long periods of time—there develops gradually, slight progress from one decade to another, a beautiful mellowness not unlike heavily-frosted hedgerows glowing in the waning winter sunshine.

Patina at its best has an apparently fathomless depth of beauty and, by the way, it hardly ever seems to need a clean! But burnish it at the repairer's and it will elude you for the next one hundred years.

When butlers became redundant after the 'Kaiser' war and un-cleaned silver was left to corrode in chests and attics, later to emerge so black that it was despatched to be polished professionally, much fine silver was reduced to a secondary condition.

Patina, once it is acquired and remains free of mishaps, continues to improve as the centuries pass. It is, perhaps, at its most magnificent on items of thick construction of the Britannia Standard era (1697-1719), but I adore it, too, as a background to the arabesque engravings of the Elizabethan period. In fact, I insist on it for antique silver of any age.

Many modern repairers and dealers think that they can produce a good patina on articles even after they have been subjected to intense heat and acid treatment. They talk nonsense, probably thinking that a dull polish instead of a bright one will produce a pleasant colour. Some misguided dealers instruct their repairers to conceal restorations with an 'antique finish' achieved by 'dark plating'; another trick is to shake a restored surface in a bag of lead shot. But these processes cannot produce a genuine antique patina and those who say otherwise have never learned to recognise it.

My personal appreciation of patina, even although it was only a sub-conscious understanding, came almost *at the outset* of my interest in silver (as is related in chapter 1) and so there is no reason why my readers should not be infected within a week or two by my apparent fetish about it.

As far as I know, no one writing about silver has ever before stressed the vital importance to collectors of being able to recognise this quality. As this expertise may enable you to pick up an unmarked Elizabethan piece at a glance and for the proverbial 'song', after hundreds of dealers and thousands of collectors have failed to recognise it, I wonder if these authors have been keeping a valuable secret to themselves!

My confidence in the recognition of a good patina, in which case, of course, there is no question of a modern repair or forgery, tends to make me lazy in my 'Routine Inspection' (chapter 15) and in consequence I fail sometimes to notice a minor antique repair. But then, I don't really worry much about very small faults providing they are themselves antique. My imagination tends to dwell upon the possible circumstances that caused each mishap. I see the banqueting hall, the table laden, admire the clothes and elegant accoutrements and wince as Henry VIII throws a standing-salt at one of his wives. Earlier that same day he had also dissolved the monasteries. . . .

When customers come to me and the conversation turns to patina, I am able to demonstrate the difference between good and bad patina. But to my disappointment they do not immediately thrill to the fine example because it requires the understanding that experience alone affords and they usually say: 'Yes, I see the difference in the colour, but I shan't be able to remember it.'

If you rub an old patina with your thumb the surface after a moment or two will feel slightly rougher or resistant while a modern surface may feel quite slippery by comparison. While trying to explain the process of recognising patination by feel to an elderly, red-nosed street trader, he retorted with withering scorn: 'blimey, governor, I can scarcely feel my glass, nowadays'. After that experience, I have felt that it was safer, when trying to help someone, to concentrate on visual recognition. Some experts consider that new surfaces have a pink appearance while old, unrestored surfaces have a steely blue look. I can recognise the latter but not the former tinge. When you have handled a hundred or more pieces of good and bad patina, something will 'click' and then you've started! You will decide that on silver of thick construction the recognisable tinge on good patination is white-grey and on items of thinner construction the tinge is blue-grey.

You must go to a specialist dealer of long standing and of great knowledge, in whom you have complete confidence. Then, put yourself unreservedly into his hands. Ask for a small item of silver, something that will fit into your pocket, perhaps a Queen Anne, Hanoverian-style, rat-tail table spoon, of glorious patina and impeccable quality throughout. If a table spoon, it should weigh about 30 ozs. Tell the dealer that you are just starting to collect and you require a piece as a model of excellence with which to compare all the other silver that you propose to inspect in the coming months.

With such an approach it would be a very mean character indeed who did not warm to the task of helping you.

Starting off on the right foot in this manner and keeping your small specimen piece always at hand wherever you go, the recognition of patina will represent an early break-through into the most important single aspect of expertise.

Silver-Gilt.

Much silver throughout the ages was gilt or parcel (partly) gilt. The difference between antique and modern gilding can be recognised by the novice at a glance (see chapter 15). It is wise to avoid all items with modern gilding for such pieces, usually have something to conceal.

11

Who Will Help Me?

There are thousands of dealers who would like to help you, who consider that they are competent to help you, but who, despite their good intentions, are as likely as not to do you a disservice.

I know a few dealers in London and the provinces to whom I could entrust you with every confidence. I would like to name such dealers for your assistance, but in doing this I would offend a greater number, many of whom are friends of mine, whose integrity is beyond doubt but whose knowledge is suspect. You must pick your own dealers wherever you live—and there are several across the Atlantic ocean whom I could recommend—but only after the most exhaustive enquiries.

One cannot learn the practical side of handling silver by reading books, but all books and articles by Richard Came of Sotheby's, Eric Delieb, Arthur Grimwade of Christie's, the late Commander G. E. P. How, Mrs G. E. P. How, C. C. Oman and Norman Penzer are invariably well worth reading.

At Christie's and Sotheby's auction rooms in London, where I hope you will be able to spend many happy hours in pursuing the policy and advice offered in chapter 14, there is expert advice 'on tap', which you must make use of if you wish to make purchases before you are reasonably experienced.

At any auction, falsified silver does, very occasionally or very frequently, depending on the expertise available to the auctioneers, slip through unnoticed. There are also a number of suspicious pieces that are hard to condemn out of hand, but which one certainly would not wish to own, not infrequently turning up under every 'hammer'.

Even although Christie's and Sotheby's, of course, handle the 'cream' of antique silver, they also have their share of third-rate pieces to dispose of.

At these two auction rooms, if you enquire at their offices, you can obtain an expert assessment of the approximate price that every lot in the sale is expected to fetch. If you pursue the matter further and are seriously considering making purchases—let's be fair—the auctioneers, two of the leading authorities in the world, will offer you their personal opinion regarding the merits of any item, or items, in which you are interested. I have found their comments extremely fair.

The metalwork department at the Victoria and Albert Museum, London, is also a boon to silver enthusiasts. Since the retirement of the great C. C. Oman from this museum the department has two experts, one specialising on silver prior to the eighteenth century, and another specialising from 1700 to modern times. These experts will examine and offer an opinion on any item that you care to take them. There is no charge for this splendid service, but they will never make valuations. You can either make an appointment to see them or call in during specific periods.

I 2

(a) What is Quality?
(b) What is its Value in 'Hard Cash'?

'Quality' is a word much used in the silver trade and it is usually mis-used. Novice collectors should be prepared for these irregularities. My first impression of the meaning of 'quality', when applied to silver by dealers, was that it was synonomous with thick or sturdy construction and the phrase 'better quality' implied, above all other considerations, a 'greater weight for size'. Subsequently, after I had heard the word employed as an adjective (example: 'it's a real 'quality' piece) I decided that 'quality' must express a 'general desirability' and (usually) something well worth buying. But the word is frequently used in sales talk and I have even heard 'rarity' (of an item) included amongst the attributes of 'quality'. There are degrees of 'quality', the usual extremes of which are termed either 'superb' or 'poor'.

As we are discussing silver we might as well write about it in the vernacular of our trade and so for the purposes of this chapter my interpretation of 'quality'—presented with profuse apologies to *The Oxford English Dictionary*—is a peculiar excellence (relating to any item of silver) caused by a number of favourable, valuable and diverse attributes, the most important of which, I think, is beauty.

Realism compels us to include good marks amongst the attributes of quality. Yet a nicer understanding could recall the craftsman's lingering inspection of the finished work, his reluctance to turn away, his compulsive return to look again and finally his glow of happiness and pride from confirmation of his artistry.

Do our eyes deceive us? Is personal taste, born of long experience, an unreliable guide? If beauty lies in the eyes of the beholder then the assembly of middle-aged hard-headed, elderly bald-headed, silver dealers—sometimes referred to as 'The boys'—sitting round the table at Christie's or Sotheby's must be consistently deceived or deceiving! The important point at issue is that all these dealers and many of the small ones too, the auctioneers, and their more senior porters, the better-educated members of the public who swarm to these important art auctions all share a remarkable unanimity of opinion as to what constitutes beauty, and this unanimity is proven invariably by the high price a beautiful piece obtains.

On the other hand, the general public as they buy their 'turn-of-the-century' junk, their fussy Victoriana, their terribly ordinary, poor quality, Georgian milk jugs and their much-restored vinaigrettes seems to suffer a conception of beauty that the patrons of the big auctions would abhor.

We cannot blame money for these extreme contrasts of taste. Although a large part of the public's purchases would not be accepted for sale at a big auction, and the remainder, mostly lumped together in 'lots' of numerous items and sold for about a quarter of cost price, their actual outlay amounts to a tragic squandering of hard-earned money, viz: tiny Edwardian silver match boxes at £3 or £4 each, simple thimbles at £2, pairs of berry spoons at £25, forged caddy spoons at £10, later embossed Georgian tankards at £150 and similar coffee pots at £350.

The explanation, I think, is that those who are privileged to be born with beautiful things around them and those whose work involves the constant handling of beautiful things and even those who are shrewd enough to buy beautiful things, grow to love and understand them. The wireless has brought the appreciation of good music into millions of homes, but the appreciation of beauty in other forms of art requires effort. That is perhaps why one quite often hears someone say: 'I don't like silver.'

In the auction rooms the quality of antique silver can be assessed in cash, but however high one's personal assessment of an outstanding piece may be, it is, from personal experience, inevitable that others assess the value even higher!

I will list the attributes of quality and place them, first in the order of preference that I think an experienced dealer considering purchasing for stock would rate them, and secondly for an experienced collector forming his personal collection.

Dealer.
1. Beauty and outstanding design.
2. Brilliant marks.
3. Crispness of design (if applicable).
4. Unspoiled patina.
5. Good weight for size.
6. Balance.

Collector.
1. Beauty and outstanding design.
2. Patina.
3. Brilliant marks.
4. Crispness of design (if applicable).
5. Good weight for size.
6. Balance.

The next useful step is to attempt to put a cash value on quality, but we will be working only on broad approximations. Let us assume that a George III coffee pot, London, 1763, is worth £1,050 and that its quality is perfect in every respect. Below, I make an attempt to estimate how the figure of £1,050 is arrived at:

> The coffee pot £20.
> Beauty, design and craftsmanship £300.
> Superb patina £210.
> Brilliant marks £250.
> Very satisfactory weight for size £180.
> Fine, contemporary Coat of Arms £100.
> Good balance £50.
> Crispness of decoration (not applicable in this instance) must be considered in conjunction with 'beauty'.

The reader may be confused when he glances at the above table for the first time and so I have tried to simplify the matter by anticipating his questions.

Q. How could anyone in their senses assess the value of a mid-Georgian coffee pot at only £20?

A.   If the general condition was so poor that it was virtually be-
      yond repair: Scrap silver stands in value at ·70p per oz: at day
      of writing.
Q.   I thought price was fixed by the age of an article.
A.   Age is certainly a very important factor of price. A good
      Queen Anne coffee pot (very rare) would certainly be worth
      very much more than a good George III pot (not so rare), but,
      on the other hand, a fine modern reproduction pot (worth
      about £60) might be worth more than a very poor antique
      example in the same style as that from which the reproduction
      was copied.
Q.   BEAUTY IS AN INTANGIBLE QUALITY. How can it be
      valued?
A.   By learning to appreciate it. You are referred back to the be-
      ginning of this chapter (para: 3).
Q.   What does a good balance imply?
A.   If I speak of tight-ropes and pretty girls with umbrellas high
      above the circus arena ... perhaps, I oversimplify. Handle
      a number of pieces of fine quality silver and you'll soon
      understand.
Q.   Do dealers really make valuations in this manner?
A.   They must work on similar lines. Certainly, they would not
      guess values. Incidentally, let me know, please, when you have
      thought of a better method of valuation.

I will now deduct from the valuation of 1,000 gns for this coffee
pot appropriate figures for lack of 'quality' in others, similar. After
considerable experimentation, the resulting 'guides', if applied realistically, provide sensible final figures for the value of any similar
coffee pot.

Note 1.   By 'similar coffee pot', we mean same style, date and
           weight.
Note 2.   No combination of faults to exceed a total of £1,030.
Note 3.   Directly deductions have reached or passed a total of
           £500, all subsequent deductions to be at the rate of 20
           per cent of estimated deduction for à particular fault.
           Deductions must commence and continue with the big-
           gest, single deduction outstanding.
Note 4.   When practising valuations on the lines outlined in the

following table, you must consider carefully the meaning of the words 'up to' and 'about'. 'Up to' permits a wide discretionary variation from the maximum deduction recommended. 'About' does not and should not suggest much room for manoeuvre.

Note 5.   The reader is entitled to wonder why we are bothering to discuss the valuation of items that, for example, have been electro-plated, embossed and de-chased, when he has been warned against buying them. It would be most encouraging for me if he were to take his question a stage further by asking: 'if the buyer knows there are serious defects, he would not think of buying, surely?'

Some dealers have been trading in both poor and fine quality silver for decades and they know what they are doing even although the vast majority of their customers do not. Auction prices, in fact, are usually more accurately predictable on poor than on superb quality items. I feel it is important that students should find their way along all the paths of the 'jungle'. The recognition and understanding of bad silver helps you to appreciate the good.

Note 6.   *It is, of course, pointless to practise valuations in this manner until you have acquired some general experience of prices on the lines suggested* (chapter 14, sec: C.2.).

Deductions (from £1,050).

1. Visible repairs   up to £1,000
2. A weak patch where, for example, a crest has been removed. This weakness could be patched over, etc.   up to £975
3. Rubbed hall-marks   up to £850
4. Absence of all hall-marks, but with contemporary, identified Coat of Arms or crest   about £750*
5. Electro-plated, concealing repairs   about £650
6. Extensive later decoration or de-chasing of such decoration   about £600

* The difference in value between marked and unmarked silver (other than spoons before say 1620) would be considerably less. Pieces with a makers' mark but with no hall-marks would be worth about one third more than a totally unmarked item.

7.	Indifferent design and craftsmanship	up to £500
8.	Poor patina	up to £500
9.	Marks missing from lid (but lid not suspect)	about £500
10.	Poor weight for size	up to £500
11.	Later initials or monogram	up to £400
12.	Poor balance	up to £200
13.	Later handle	up to £150
14.	Later crest or coat of arms	up to £100

Examples of comparing the price-difference between the specimen coffee pot, valued at 1,000gns, with other similar coffee pots.

Example 1.

3.	Marks a little rubbed	deduct £200
1.	Slight antique repair	deduct £150
13.	Later handle	deduct £150
7.	Attractive but not spectacular. Deduct 20% of £250 = £50	deduct £ 50
14.	Later crest. Deduct 20% of £100 = £20	deduct £ 20

Total deductions £570

Value of coffee pot therefore £1,050 less £570 = £480.

Example 2.

5.	Electro-plated	deduct £650
8.	Poor patina. Deduct 20% of £500 = £100	deduct £100
3.	Rather rubbed but decipherable. Deduct 20% of £375 = £75	deduct £ 75
1.	Slight indications of repairs even after E.P. Deduct 20% of £250 = £50	deduct £ 50

Total deductions £875

Value of coffee pot therefore £1,050 less £875 = £175.

SO QUALITY REALLY DOES COUNT, DOESN'T IT?

13

Marks that are Valuable and/or Confusing

Provided that you have good eyes or a powerful magnifying glass and a copy, bought or borrowed, of the tome under discussion, it should not take more than a few minutes to assimilate the lay-out of the 750 pages contained in the second edition of Sir Charles Jackson's *English Goldsmiths and Their Marks* and, as they are self-explanatory, learn the broad rules for identifying marks. But a provincial, general dealer of my acquaintance, whom we can call Mick, had never learned to read, and was therefore mystified by the numerous date-cycles and assay-offices, and was sadly handicapped when it came to pricing his silver wares. I do not think he had even the assistance of knowing what any item had cost him. Quite early in my acquaintanceship with him I suspected that he was offering stolen goods. Thus I was unable to take advantage of his unique terms of business in which he enjoyed a rapid turnover: he charged £3 per ounce for every item that bore a king's head, £2 for a queen's head and if no head at all the cost was only £1 per ounce. Accordingly all silver made before 1784, when the sovereign's head was first struck on English silver, was sold at the same price as the modern. Few members of the public benefited from Mick's price structure for invariably there was a throng of dealers jockeying for favourable positions round his stall whenever he was expected.

One day I noticed a couple of detectives by Mick's stall and they seemed unimpressed by the alternating flow of 'blarney' or indignation, interspersed with impassioned appeals to well-known 'celestial personages' to vindicate his testimony, before 'the fuzz', as he used

PLATE I. James II two handled porringer and cover, chased in the Chinese taste with figures, plants, exotic birds and buildings, on circular moulded foot and with scroll beaded handles, the cover similarly decorated to the body and with open acanthus bud finial. 6 in. high, 23 oz., London, 1688, maker's mark a goose in dotted circle, the cover unmarked.

Note: This item of exceptional quality obtained £3,500 at public auction, despite the absence of marks on the lid, at a time when the prices of ordinary items of antique silver were at their nadir.

By courtesy of Messrs Christie, Manson & Woods.

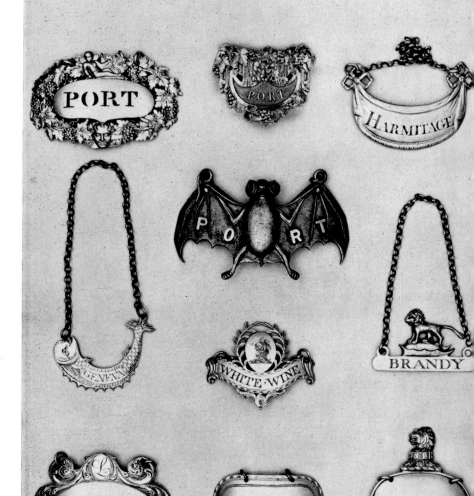

PLATE 2. *Top centre*: Silver-gilt label of crescent shape surrounded by chased borders of vine leaves and bunches of grapes surmounted by a lion's mask and skin, the centre titled on granulated ground for Port, 2¾ in. wide, by Paul Storr, London 1815. *Top left*: Silver-gilt shaped oval label, pierced for Port within a chased and pierced border of matted vine leaves and bunches of grapes, the reclining figure of Cupid above, and a Bacchanal mask below, by George Purse, London, 1818. *Top right*: Label in the form of a ribbon-tied drapery festoon with fringed lower border, engraved for Harmitage (sic), by Boulton and Fothergill, Birmingham, 1775. Hermitage was a claret from the Rhone Valley famous in the eighteenth and nineteenth centuries. *Second centre*: Label in the form of a bat, the typically displayed wings matted and applied with the title Port, 3 in. wide, unmarked, early nineteenth century. *Second left*: Label in the form of a leaping dolphin, engraved for Geneva with scales, unmarked, possibly provincial, early nineteenth century. Geneva was an early spelling of gin, derived from the French genièure (juniper), as was the Swiss city. *Third centre*: Label engraved for White Wine on a wriggle-work scroll-shaped section with foliate spray below and crested oval cartouche above within pierced laurel branches, by Susannah Barker, London circa 1780. *Second right*: Silver-gilt label, engraved on an oblong section for Brandy below the crest of the Earls of Shrewsbury, maker's mark R.L., I.D., London, 1801. *Third left*: Oval label engraved for Brandy below a bright-cut scrolling foliate mantle incorporating the initial L., by James Hyde, London, circa 1790. *Fourth centre*: Label of oblong form, engraved for Mountain, within pricked wriggle-work and bright-cut borders, by Susannah Barker, London, 1791. Mountain is a sweet wine from the mountains of Malaga. *Third right*: Oval label, pierced within a plain moulded border for Champagne, and surmounted by a cast and chased crest, by John Reily, London, 1823.

These illustrations reproduced by courtesy of Messrs. Sotheby & Co.

PLATE 3. *Top row* (left to right): Caddy-spoon in form of eagle's feather. By Joseph Taylor, Birmingham, 1793, 3 in. in length. Silver-gilt. Caddy-spoon known as the giant mandarin type. Maker's mark E. F., London, 1831, weight 1.8 ozs., 3 3/16th in. in length. Caddy-spoon possibly commemorating the conclusion of the war with France. Oval filigree bowl enriched with figures of two finely modelled doves holding olive-branch which is flanked by a fleur-de-lys and the royal crown of England. Unmarked, circa 1816, 2 7/8th in. in length. *Bottom row* (left to right): Caddy-spoon in form of acorn. London, 1811, by E. Morley, 2 5/8th in. in length. Caddy-spoon with filigree centre to bowl. It has been suggested that the letters in cypher form the surname of Nelson and that the engraving on the front of the handle is meant to denote ship's hawsers. By Samuel Pemberton, Birmingham, 1807, 2 11/16th in. in length. A leaf-shaped caddy-spoon with the bowl embossed with 'colours', pennon, cannon, drum, fife, bayonets, axes and cannon-'ram rods'. Presumably, this spoon commemorates a battle. Maker's mark W. W., Birmingham, 1804, 2 7/8th in. in length. The bowl of this caddy-spoon is shaped like the foot of a horse and the handle like a horse's leg, surmounted by a hoof. But the author does not consider that the goldsmith had much idea of a horse's normal conformation. By W. Lea & Co., Birmingham, 1821, 2 9/16th in. in length.

The above rare caddy spoons are reproduced by courtesy of The Colchester and Essex Museum. They form part of the museum's important collection of some 300 specimens.

PLATE 4.

Soup Tureen and Cover. The body of bombé form on four shell feet with rococo cartouche engraved with a coat of arms flanked by festoons of shells, the handles formed as boldly modelled dolphins with recurving tails balanced on the other side by bunches of bulrushes, with strapwork and rosette ring the domed cover with reed-and-tie rim chased with shells at intervals, surmounted by a realistically modelled crab on circular cartouche flanked by scalework panels, bordered by festoons of shells on matted ground with small rococo cartouches engraved with a crest. London, 1737, by John Edwards, 141oz.

By courtesy of Messrs Christie, Manson & Woods.

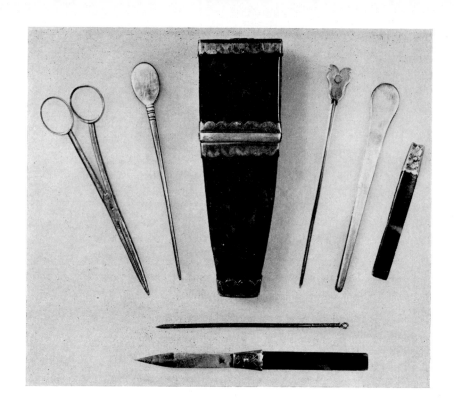

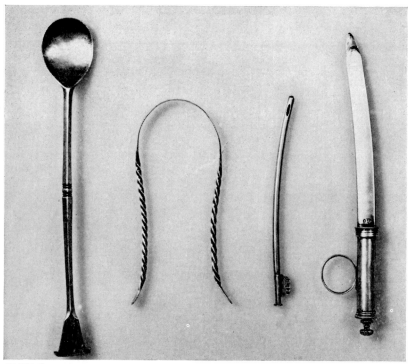

PLATE 5.

PLATE 6.

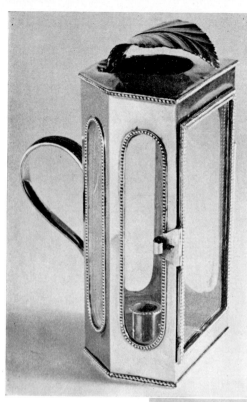

PLATE 7. Sheffield Plate. Lantern. Unmarked, circa 1795, about 6½ in. high.

PLATE 8. Sheffield Plate. Lidded Tankard with the maker's mark of Henry Tudor struck four times in similar manner to silver marks and possibly intended to deceive the unwary. Circa 1760, about 7 in. high.

Reproduced by courtesy of Sheffield Museums.

PLATE 9. The rare 'drawback' mark struck with the full London hall-marks—showing the sovereign's head incuse, looking to the left—for the year 1785.

Reproduced by courtesy of Messrs. Sotheby & Co.

PLATE 10. Rare strainer in 'Sheffield Plate' with tubular, tapering handle. Circa 1780, about 8 in. long.

Reproduced by courtesy of Sheffield Museums.

PLATE 11. Forgery in 'Sheffield Plate' of Bank of England Britannia Dollar, 1804

PLATE 12. 'Sheffield Plate'. Pair of Tapersticks, with Corinthian columns, entwined husk pattern, on square base decorated with garlands and shells. By John Winter & Co., circa 1770, about 5½ in.

Reproduced by courtesy of Sheffield Museums.

PLATE 13. Alterations from a George III tablespoon. The apostle finial and rat-tails have been added and the bowls reshaped. Forgeries of this nature may still be seen amongst the stock of ignorant or dishonest dealers.

Reproduced by courtesy of Worshipful Company of Goldsmiths.

PLATE 14. Illegal alterations from spoons. The bowls have been removed and prongs substituted. The solder line is just visible on the stem of the upper one. The ends have been reshaped.

Reproduced by courtesy of Worshipful Company of Goldsmiths.

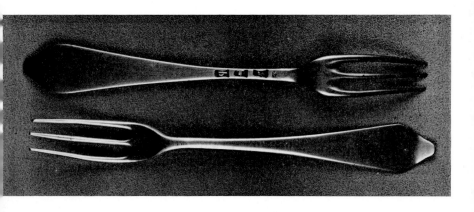

PLATE 15. Six tobacco boxes showing typical coats-of-arms within cartouches of the period 1685-1725.

Top (left to right) c.1700., c.1685., c.1695.

Bottom. c.1725., c.1705., c.1700.

Reproduced by courtesy of Messrs. Sotheby & Co.

PLATE 16. A Charles I instrument for measuring chords, and embracing a six inch ruler, engraved: 'D. D: Principi: R. Delamain. Aetatis Suae 12 Anno 1639'. Later engraving on the other side: 'John Harvey Esqr 1732'. Richard Delamain, a father mathematician, dedicated his 'Grammelogia' to King Charles and was appointed tutor to the king in mathematics. Delamain presented a silver ring sundial to the Duke of York but the recipient of the gift illustrated remains untraced. The discovery of this instrument is recorded in chapter 5.

In the collection of Maj: H. B. McCance.

PLATE 17. Transposed hall-marks (London, 1765) on a ewer.

Reproduced by courtesy of Worshipful Company of Goldsmiths.

PLATE 18. Forged hall-marks (London, 1808) on a mustard pot.

Reproduced by courtesy of Worshipful Company of Goldsmiths.

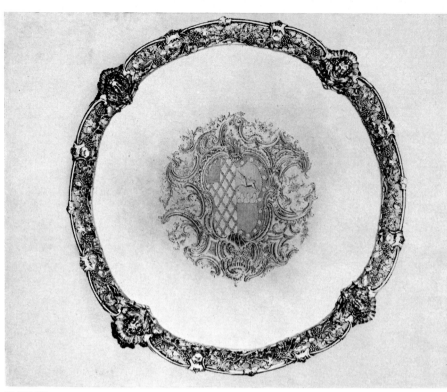

PLATE 19.

PLATE 20.

PLATE 21.

PLATE 19. George II salver on vine decorated cast supports, the similar pierced border also chased with shellwork and masks, the centre engraved with contemporary armorials in a rococo cartouche, 27½ ins. diam. Marked on base and border, by William Cripps, London, 1754, 226.5 oz.

PLATE 20. George I teapot of octagonal pear shape, with a moulded border at the shoulders, engraved with contemporary armorials in a cartouche of scrolling foliage, strap-work and a shell on a scale ground, faceted bird neck spout and domed cover with baluster finial, 7½ in. high, marked on base and cover, by Francis Garthorne, London, 1723, 26.25 oz.

PLATE 21. Pair of table candlesticks with reeded and fluted column stems, on crested double tiered octagonal bases bordered with gadroons and ovolos, the fixed nozzles similarly decorated, 9¼ in. high, maker's mark D.B. a star above, an annulet below, London, 1694, 37.7 oz. *Centre*: Queen Anne baluster hot-milk jug, engraved with contemporary armorials in a lozenge with mask above within scroll and foliate decoration, the wood handle at right angles to the short moulded spout, domed lid, on circular foot, 6¾ in. high, marked on base, by Charles Overing, London, 1710, 10 oz.

Reproduced by courtesy of Messrs. Sotheby & Co.

PLATE 22. *Left*: James I wine cup with tall baluster stem and shallow bowl, the spreading foot decorated with lappets on pounced ground, the bowl with similar ornament between bands of stamped lozenges, 6½ in. high, maker's mark R over W in a shaped shield, London, 1618, 6.3 oz. *Right*: Charles II porringer of baluster form with caryatid scroll handles, the lower part of the body chased with poppy-heads and tulips, 3¼ in. high, maker's mark W.N., four pellets below, in a heart-shaped shield, London, 1671, 6.45 oz.

Reproduced by courtesy of Messrs. Sotheby & Co.

to call them, led him away to a waiting car. Mick, as if well experienced with this type of inconvenience, left in a dignified way, finally displaying a resigned composure which was in marked contrast to the very evident agitation of several of his neighbours and erstwhile regular customers. I do not know what became of Mick nor how he is now employed. He had told me more than once that as a boy he had dearly wanted to become a priest. . . .

Considering that Sir Charles Jackson began his tome in 1887, its second edition appearing as long ago as 1921, it is remarkable that silver experts of today have little of real importance to add and comparatively few corrections to make to it. 'Jackson's' seems likely to remain the outstanding reference book for antique silver until at least the end of the twentieth century, and as so little silver of merit or collectors' interest is being made in this century it could possibly survive for ever.

However, I do recall meeting a few initial problems when looking up 'marks', both assay and makers'. These, together with the mention of marks of special interest and some which are unrecorded in 'Jackson's' and often unrecognised in the trade, should be of service.

My first surprise when studying assay marks was to see the head of a lion described as that of a leopard. This irregularity probably originated because the ancient heraldic term 'leopart' means a 'lion passant guardant' and a full explanation is given in 'Jackson's' on page 51. Indeed, the animal's head with its smug expression, depicted on very early plate, reminds me of a tom-cat ruminating, perhaps, upon his amatory adventures and certainly not on plagues and fires!

It may have been a fire that caused the disappearance of the records of makers' marks some time after 1677 and so, although 'Jackson's' portrays hundreds of early goldsmiths' symbols or initials, we know but few of the makers' actual names before 1697.

The temporary departure from the sterling standard (18 dwts of alloy to 11 ozs 2 dwts of silver) in 1696, in order to prevent goldsmiths from grabbing the coinage—a cheaper and already refined source of silver—with which to fashion their plate, and the establishment of the so-called Britannia Standard (10 dwts of alloy to 11 ozs 10 dwts of silver) presents the student not only with marks of quite a new style (the figure of Britannia and the lion's head erased) but with three other points to consider:

65

1. Coincidental with the Britannia marks, goldsmiths were required to stamp their personal mark with the first two letters of their surname instead of with their initials or symbol.

2. The provincial assay-offices were not allowed to use the new Britannia Standard marks ('Jackson's' pages 18-19) until 1700. At Newcastle*, for no certain reason, the goldsmiths were obliged to wait until 1702. So, for some years, provincial goldsmiths were obliged to confine their business to items on special order. On such wares of this period (1696-1700)—if there were any marks at all—one finds a maker's mark and very, very occasionally the words either Sterling or Britannia. What a 'feather-in-the-cap' for a beginner if he found an example of these latter marks. If it subsequently turned out that his prize did not originate from the provinces between 1696 and 1700 but from either Chester, 1609-1695, or Cork, circa 1710, he would not experience great financial disappointment!

3. After the sterling standard was restored in 1719, the use of the Britannia Standard remained optional and is sometimes still employed today, often on reproductions of items in vogue in the 1696-1719 period. Beginners must take care for occasionally the modern date letter has been deliberately and illegally erased to deceive the inexperienced.

Attention must be drawn to the curious antics of the lion passant at Newcastle between 1722 and 1728, for sometimes he faced to the left and sometimes to the right.† The sovereign's head in the first two years of its inception, 1784, and 1785, at London, Exeter, Newcastle, Chester, Birmingham, Sheffield and Edinburgh was engraved as an intaglio. Subsequently it was engraved as a cameo until omitted after 1889. In 1797 at the Birmingham assay office, after the duty payable on wrought silver had been doubled, the sovereign's head was sometimes struck twice. This double mark seems to have been a unique form of receipt for duty paid.

The town mark of the York Assay was often omitted and the same omission is often noted on other sets of provincial silver marks,

---

* It is doubtful if there was a properly conducted assay office at Newcastle until 1702. Up to this year, goldsmiths made and struck their own marks.

† John Dowthwaite of Newcastle, who worked between 1666 and 1673 punched his wares with a lion facing to the left. His apprentice, Francis Batty—the elder—married Dowthwaite's widow and probably inherited his late master's set of punches. John Wilkinson, circa 1660, also used a lion facing left.

notably at Newcastle and Exeter. About 1800 and later, and usually on smaller items, one frequently notices incomplete sets of marks assayed at London and the provinces. The leopard's head, for example, was often missing at London and elsewhere where it was used.

No silversmith of the nineteenth century, it seems, was more meticulous than Nathaniel Mills in insisting that his work was fully marked; while Samuel Pemberton, also using the Birmingham assay office, was as indolent in this respect as he was industrious in production. I once saw a nutmeg grater of superb quality made by the former and presumably sent to be assayed shortly after the death of George IV; the assay official had stamped the head of George IV on the lid and the head of William IV on the base and omitted a date letter on both sections. Had the official been celebrating and decided to puzzle posterity for a joke? I have no doubt that your guess to account for these irregularities would be as good as mine.

Up to the third quarter of the eighteenth century, the assay officials and goldsmiths of Dublin, as if reflecting the happy-go-lucky approach to life of many Irish people, seemed consistently unpredictable in their use of marks. Thus, the beginner who is still unable to determine date by style is liable to become greatly confused. As I write, I am looking at a Dublin helmet cream jug, circa 1768, struck with one Hibernia mark, *two* crowned harp punches and lacking both a date letter and a maker's mark. On this item, the student by referring to 'Jackson's' (page 613) would have expected one Hibernia punch, one crowned harp, a date letter and a maker's mark.

Among the seven or eight thousand makers' marks illustrated in 'Jackson's' there are, of course, a number of mistakes and, as one would expect after all the research of the last three or four decades, the names of a considerable number of goldsmiths who are not recorded therein have been brought to light. The Wine Label Circle (Hon. Sec. The Rev. E. W. Whitworth, Stadhampton Rectory, Oxon.) has accomplished much valuable research in this respect and has (privately) printed papers illustrating over one hundred makers' marks that are either unrecorded or unidentified in 'Jackson's'. As examples of wine labels have not yet been found before about 1730, these long lists of recently identified makers date only from that period. Presumably all these goldsmiths produced these attractive little accessories to glass decanters. Our Georgian ancestors certainly enjoyed a wide variety of wines with exciting names, but most of these have now disappeared from modern wine-merchants' lists. In *The Antique Collector* of April, 1968, Mr R. B. C. Ryall, a member of the Wine Label Circle, wrote a highly informative treatise on this subject entitled *On Collecting Wine Labels*.

My friend, and customer of the early fifties, Mr J. W. Clark, L.D.S., R.C.S., of Newcastle Upon Tyne, has spent much time researching the Newcastle goldsmiths and his investigations extend back to 1185. In about 1959, Bill Clark discovered and identified the chalice and paten at Ilderton, dated 1583, and made by Valentine Baker. This is seventy-three years earlier than any item of Newcastle plate known to Sir Charles Jackson. In the *Archaeolagia Aeliana*, 4th series, vol. XLVII (published in 1969 by Northumberland Press Ltd) Bill Clark's article *The Copper Plate of the Goldsmiths' Company of Newcastle Upon Tyne*—The copper plate upon which all the Newcastle makers' marks are impressed from 1702—is invaluable to any student specialising in Newcastle silver of the eighteenth and nineteenth centuries.

I quote an extract from his kind hurried letter to me of December 19th, 1951:

'the mug is interesting. The maker's mark is an overstamp. The rest of the marks are undoubtedly 1757 (I have tankards of that year by John Langlands). Pinkney commenced his apprenticeship in 1767. Admitted 1778 and set up on his own account in that year. Scott commenced his apprenticeship in 1760. Admitted 1781. Went into partnership with Pinkney. The partnership was dissolved in 1790. They were apprentices together. They worked for Langlands together. I'll bet this mug, somehow, stuck to them when they went into business together and their mark was stamped over Langland's. Pinkney was a man of substance. He had married money in a big way—and retired at the age of 46. He died 1825 aged 73. Scott was the son of a blacksmith. His mother was a parson's daughter—and his son became a parson. He died 1793 and left very little. Dear, dear, dear, I rhyme on about these Newcastle 'smiths as though I knew them. They were a great set of lads and the wangles they got up to were nobody's business.'

The mug, referred to in this letter, might have confused even an experienced collector for it was dated 1757 and it bore the mark of makers who did not start operations until 1781!

With Bill Clark's letter of 1951, he enclosed a list of errors noted in the Newcastle section of 'Jackson's'. When these errors are compared with the numerous entries of makers' marks, you will realise how little he considered was at fault.

> Page 360. Footnote. Alter 1668 to 1674/5. Then cross out the whole lot.
> Lines 6, 7, 8, 9, 10, 11 and 12—Alter Wm Ramsay to Wm Robinson 11.
> Lines 13, 14 and 16. Alter Wm Robinson to Wm Ramsay.
> Line 18. Alter date to 1696 and name to Wm Ramsay. Mark*
> Line 22. Alter Wm Robinson to Wm Ramsay jnr. Mark*
> * These are probably the marks of Wm Ramsay jnr.
> Page 369.
> Line 26. William Robinson 1. Alter date of death to 1654.
> Line 28. William Robinson 11. Earliest mention should be 1657.
>   Date of death should be 1674/5.
> Line 39. William Ramsay, jnr. Date of death should be 1701.
> Page 481. Cross out 'or Wm Robinson' at foot of page.

Further extracts from another letter from Bill Clark are well worth recording:

> 'I like old Parsival. In my searches in the old minute books of the Associated Company I find: "Jan. 6th, 1681. Parsival Soulsby fined againe for not paying ye former fine. 3s. 4d. Paid in full." And he is fined "againe for gross abuse to the company generally in getting upon the table with his foot and striking violently with his cane at Christopher Lodge endeavouring to beat out his brains and this not to be abated. Paid in full 3s. 4d."
> There's another nice one about him. He complained that Wm Husband called his wife "an idle clashing queane'. That translated means "an idle, gossipping whore". These old boys had a picturesque turn of language.'

Although there is not a lot to alter in 'Jackson's' so far as Newcastle is concerned, considerable doubts exist regarding the marks attributed to Lincoln ('Jackson's' page 441). Only the I over M (page 441 line 4) is accepted as certainly of Lincoln origin. The device of the *fleur de lys*, the emblem of the Virgin Mary, to whom is dedicated the city's cathedral, is contained in the arms of Lincoln, but the same device is also incorporated in the arms of many other places. The marks attributed to Belfast, circa 1780-1800 ('Jackson's' page 712) have been proven incorrect by Mr Victor F. Denaro. In his article in *Antique Dealer and Collectors' Guide*, September, 1968 entitled 'Maltese Silver and the Red Hand of Ulster', he explains that like Churchill's famous V sign, the open hand is regarded in Malta as a symbol of defiance and in the period 1780-1800 the island was either under threat or under occupation by the French. He states that the marks M and R ('Jackson's' page 712, lines 1, 2, 4, 5) represented two of the three standards of silver wrought in Malta during this period while unidentified makers' marks tentatively attributed by 'Jackson's' to Belfast have also been identified and named as Maltese silversmiths. Finally, the 'Red Hand of Ulster' incorporated in the royal arms of Ulster is a right hand. The symbol shown in 'Jackson's' is a *left hand*.

When I first encountered the 'registry of designs' mark (already mentioned in chapter 7) and not recorded in 'Jackson's' I was as nonplussed as when I first saw \English hall-marks with an additional device on foreign silver imported into this country towards the end of the nineteenth century (see 'Jackson's' page 27).

I was irritated with myself for failing to realise for several years that the London date cycles, starting with that of 1716, and in each cycle of twenty letters omitting either J or I, U or V and W, X, Y, Z, invariably commenced therefore of the sixth year of every second decade (viz: 1716, 1736, 1756, etc). With the aid of my fingers drumming laboriously on whatever solid surface lay within my reach—and to the possible alarm of anyone watching this seemingly irrational performance—I could have placed a precise date to any clear London marks, on or after 1716, from the very outset of my interest in antique silver.

Much of this chapter may seem to be 'third-form stuff' for those already familiar with these idosyncracies but the beginner may be lucky enough to avoid mistakes and it is for his benefit that I include examples which may be common knowledge to others. In mentioning a number of marks whose rarity greatly enhances the value of any fine piece of silver that bears them, I must again warn 'third-formers' that it is extremely dangerous to purchase anything except from the most reputable, experienced sources until you have completed the studies outlined in chapter 14 of this book. My purpose is to prepare you first so that you can reap the rewards in six months' time. This is not a long sentence and with exceptional industry some remission might be earned.

It is a far cry from Nipper and Bath racecourse in 1946 to a discussion about silver marks, but however irrelevant Nipper may be to our current subject I must illustrate the risks and opportunities that you will encounter as student dealers or collectors. On the other hand, I would like to stress that this and other stories in my book do not reflect the character of the vast majority of runners and dealers, for in the main they are a responsible section of society.

To return to Bath: I was about to place a bet in Tattersalls when I felt a sudden lightening of my race-glass case that was hung upon a shoulder. My glasses had vanished from within the case and a tubby, ugly little man with a suspicious bulge at the back of his unbuttoned raincoat was hurrying away towards the stands. As I caught up and placed a hand on his shoulder, he turned to face me with a splendid show of nonchalance and a smile so nice that it transformed his ugly features.

'I have reason to think that you have stolen my glasses,' I said. 'You're mistaken, "guv",' he said pleasantly. An embarrassing indecision assailed me. The suspicious bulge under the raincoat had vanished and I was about to ask if he would permit my searching him when I spotted my glasses lying behind his heels. Undoubtedly, under cover of the raincoat, he had deftly lowered my glasses by the straps to the ground. I had neither seen nor heard this crafty move.

Even today I am not a fully paid up member of the permissive society and I had little hesitation in escorting Nipper to the racecourse police hut. He accepted the inevitable with good humour and even tried to crack a joke. By this time I was wondering what good I thought I was doing and I was grateful for his total lack of animosity towards his captor.

In court next morning, as Nipper stood in the dock after a night in the cells, all his jauntiness had vanished and above all, I was saddened by his demeanour of utter loneliness. It was this loneliness and not his general ugliness that even now remains vividly in my memory. At the time, I wondered about his background, what chance he had had in a life probably isolated from human affection and what I could say on his behalf. He seemed about the same age as I, but obviously fate had been much kinder to me from the moment of our conception.

The case against him went much better than I could have anticipated. The defence confined the issue to two points:

'Did you see your glasses drop to the ground?'

'No.'

'Did you hear your glasses drop to the ground?'

'No.'

Nipper was given the 'benefit of the doubt' and acquitted. In confidence I was told before I left the court buildings that Nipper had thirty-five other convictions for similar offences and was a very lucky man on this occasion.

Nipper was celebrating in the racecourse bar later that same day when he spotted me and insisted on buying me a drink.

'You was real fair, "guv",' he said.

'I told the truth and I'm glad it helped.'

He looked disbelievingly at me, almost affronted momentarily, then laughed as if I had made a huge joke. One drink led to another and I found much humanity and tolerance in my new friend.

It was eighteen years before I saw Nipper again and then I did not recognise him until it was all much too late. 'I know you, "guv",' said Nipper, stopping when he saw me in 'Collectors Corner'. 'It's my dear old friend, Mr Luddington,' he informed an equally disreputable looking companion. I shook Nipper by the hand warmly enough but my efforts to recognise him were obviously unconvincing. Nipper tried to help me: 'You know, we met down the west country a long time back.'

It was true. There was something vaguely familiar about this tubby, ugly little man and I concluded quite confidently that he must have been an auction-room acquaintance at the west country sales.

'What are you doing up this way?' I asked.

'In the antique lark, like you, and I'll be doing you a bit of good.'

A week later, Nipper arrived with an important item of silver and, even more exciting, it bore the rare and valuable drawback mark. There seemed no *rational* explanation to account for a fully marked item of such importance being brought to me by a down-at-heel yet fairly experienced runner. Certainly the piece was worth several hundred pounds.

'Very interesting,' I said, 'I hope I can afford it.'

'Just forty nicker to you, "guv", one good turn deserves another.'

Now, of course, my misgivings were confirmed—the whole affair stank to high heaven. What on earth was he talking about good turns for? And how could he, with all his auction experience, possibly value such an item at only forty pounds? But because I was greedy, confused and slow-witted, I was reluctant to let such an opportunity slip by. 'I'd like it very much, but I must know who you're running for. I must check up on that point.'

Nipper's face fell. There was a pause before he spoke: 'Let's forget about the questions, "guv", then you can have it for twenty nicker.'

'I'm not interested,' I said with emphasis.

A second 'runner'—a young man who has since fallen off the antique bandwagon and disappeared—was hanging around listening and looking while I talked to Nipper. Now, more politely, but with a face tensed with excitement, he addressed me: 'May I butt in? I'd like to buy that piece for twenty pounds as you don't want it.' I shrugged my shoulders and the two men walked away together.

Nipper avoided me after this incident but he remained a regular visitor to the London markets and as his business seemed to me to be of a legitimate nature I kept my mouth shut.

Four months elapsed and then while glancing through a catalogue before inspecting silver in an auction room, I spotted an illustration of Nipper's drawback-marked piece. So everything had been above board after all and it seemed that I had behaved idiotically! In order to punish myself still further I felt compelled to ask at the office what price they considered this item would obtain. I was told that the lot in question had been withdrawn, but they declined to give me an explanation for this action. This, I am ashamed to say, made me feel much happier for at the time I gave scant thought to the other people involved.

After the sale I asked the auctioneer why this item had been withdrawn. With amusement he told me that it was one of many pieces stolen in a big and much publicised robbery about two years before. The piece, I learned, with its value much enhanced in an inflationary era, had already been restored to its rightful owner whom I knew, and who happened to appear as I spoke with the auctioneer.

When I explained how I had encountered his interesting piece some months before, the owner asked me to contact the police in case Nipper could lead them on to bigger fry. I should have known that Nipper would never have given anyone away under any circumstances. The police asked me to give them a ring when I next saw Nipper and I agreed to this very distasteful request.

I soon saw Nipper in a market and I told him what I had promised to do. I besought him, with all the clumsy persuasion at my command, to go to the police before they came to him. He left me horrified and I heard him complain to a nearby stallholder as he went: ' "grassed" by my oldest friend,' were the actual words he used.

Oldest friend? If he really thought of me as his 'oldest friend' then he must be one of the loneliest men in all the world. Thus my memory was jogged and I suppose it was inevitable that shortly afterwards I would recall how he and I had met originally at Bath in 1946.

Nipper was not charged with any offence over this more recent incident. The police thought that his handling of the stolen property was more accidental than intentional. All in all, they were very pleased with him in recent years. They hoped that his experience with the stolen item would not deter him from continuing his new business of 'running'. It didn't, but I think he has now moved out of London. Good luck to you, Nipper, wherever you may be.

The drawback mark is still unknown to a majority of collectors and small dealers. It is not unlike the Britannia mark at first glance but as Richard Came of Sotheby's has most kindly allowed me to reproduce a magnificent photograph of it (plate 10), it is unnecessary to describe its form in detail. There is no illustration of this valuable collectors' mark in 'Jackson's' and for some reason or other it was discontinued within eight months of its inception on December 1st, 1784, when an act ('Jackson's' page 21, para: 4) gave relief from duty to manufacturing exporters of gold and silver articles by allowing them to draw back the duty they had already paid on goods destined for export. The mark was stamped at the assay office to indicate that duty had been repaid. It is possible that for the purpose of promoting export sales the concession of 1784

THE MARKS OF HESTER BATEMAN
APPEARING IN THE REGISTERS AT GOLDSMITHS HALL

PART I

No	MARK	WIDTH	DATE ENTERED	REMARKS
1	HB	3·2 mm	16 APR. 1761	
2	HB	5·725 mm	9 JAN. 1771	A VERY LARGE PUNCH, PROB. INTENDED FOR LARGER PIECES OF PLATE. UNLIKELY THAT THIS PUNCH WOULD HAVE BEEN USED ON WINE LABELS.
3	HB	6·56 mm	17 JUNE 1774	AS FOR MARK No.2
4	HB	4 mm	3 DEC. 1774	
5	HB	6·89 mm	5 JUNE 1776	AS FOR MARK No.2
6	HB	4·59 mm	21 FEB. 1778	
7	HB	4·59 mm	25 NOV. 1781	
8	HB	2·24 mm	28 JUNE 1787	A VERY SMALL PUNCH. MAY HAVE BEEN INTENDED FOR TINY FRAGILE PIECES OF SILVER.
9	HB	4·74 mm	3 AUG. 1787	THIS IS THE PUNCH WHICH APPEARS ON PIECES ALSO BEARING THE KING'S HEAD.

THE FOLLOWING MARKS, ALTHOUGH NOT REGISTERED AT GOLDSMITHS HALL, ARE BELIEVED TO BE HESTER BATEMAN

PART 2

MARK	WIDTH	MARK	WIDTH	MARK	WIDTH
HB	4·75 mm	HB	3·75 mm	HB	3·5 mm

FIGURE 2. *Reproduced by courtesy of The Wine Label Circle.*

proved insufficiently attractive to goldsmiths so that virtually no silver was exported from this country. An act of 1890 terminated the 'drawback' concession.

The goldsmiths of England may have inspired today's world-wide confidence in British banking traditions. Many of our goldsmiths were bankers and no trade in modern history can have produced so many distinguished men. A significant number of goldsmiths were ennobled, not only for valuable service in the highest public offices but sometimes, also, for their valour and competence on the field of battle. The terribly harsh penalties on those who disgraced the fraternity did not encourage 'wide boys'.

The form of a goldsmith's mark can even by itself, after the student has had a few weeks' experience, sometimes indicate the approximate date of stamping. Some mark of identification has been compulsory since 1363, but as we know already, the relevant statute was frequently ignored. Up to the middle of the sixteenth century almost all makers identified themselves with a symbol by reason of the general illiteracy of the times, and thereafter even until 1696, while most punched initials, others continued with a symbol, and it was not unusual for both initials and symbols to be contained in one mark. From 1696 to 1720 it was compulsory for the first two letters of the surname to be used and thereafter, continuing until the present day, initials of individuals or companies have been employed. From about 1730 there seemed a general tendency to reduce the size of makers' marks. Most women goldsmiths of the first half of the eighteenth century contained their initials within a diamond shaped shield.

When dealers and collectors vie with each other to acquire items of silver made by certain makers because of the outstanding merit of their craftsmanship or, maybe, just because they chance to be fashionable, such pieces obviously command inflated prices. We must place Paul Lamerie*, entered 1712, at the top of the 'inflated price league'. His work averages about five times the price of his contemporaries including Pierre Platel, to whom Lamerie was apprenticed. Silver from Peter and Jonathon Bateman's* (entered 1790 in partnership) factory reflects no exceptional craftsmanship yet seems to average about three times as much as that of other makers of the period because, as Jonathon died within a few months of the commencement of business, the partners' work is quite rare and, of course, the brothers were the sons of fashionable Hester. The work of Paul Storr*, entered 1793, and Hester Bateman,* entered 1761 (?), is inflated in price by about two and a half times and the former's popularity seems to be fully justified. Frederick Kandler,* entered 1735, and a most worthy contemporary of the great Lamerie, may cost twice as much as most of his rivals while the work of Nathaniel Mills* and Mathew Boulton,* both entering at Birmingham in the years 1826 and 1773 respectively, will command about half as much again as that of their contemporaries. John Edwards, who entered at London in 1723 (in partnership at that time with George Pitches), whom some consider to be the equal of Lamerie and Frederick Kandler is not yet fashionable.

Smaller and less important items by these popular goldsmiths, excluding Nathaniel Mills who concentrated his output on small items of fine quality, usually encourage prices in excess of my suggested ratios of inflation because less affluent and far more numerous but equally eager collectors compete for ownership of the coveted marks.

If when comparing marks, be they makers' or hall-marks, with their reproductions in 'Jackson's', the student notes slight discrepancies while still confident that he is on the right line of research, it could be that the marks on the silver being examined have been subject either to the ravages of time, faulty punching, overstamping, laxity by the die-sinker or a combination of two or more of these possibilities. Furthermore, I have no doubt that in many instances Sir Charles Jackson scrutinised several slight variations of the same mark and then instructed his penman to depict a mean average of these variations. Recently, I owned a silver and mother-of-pearl snuff box of Sheffield origin by James Law, assayed about 1790 but without a date letter. All marks were so distorted that I was obliged to seek guidance from the appropriate assay office before I was convinced

---

* The makers' marks of the six most popular goldsmiths mentioned above will be found in 'Jackson's' as follows:
Paul Lamerie: page 168 line 7, page 172 line 10, page 177 line 22, page 184 lines 8 and 22, page 200 line 7.
Peter and Jonathon Bateman: page 221 line 7.
Paul Storr: page 224 line 2, page 228 line 23, page 230 line 5.
Hester Bateman: page 216 line 25, page 217 line 13, page 220 line 23.
Nathaniel Mills: page 410 lines 3 and 5, page 411 line 1.
Matthew Boulton: page 408 lines 1, 5, 18, 21, page 409 line 5.

that the item was not colonial with forged English marks.

A study of colonial silver, as indicated in chapter 7, is beyond the scope of this course and, since much of it is wrought from substandard silver it is liable, if less than a hundred years old, to be seized by Goldsmiths' Hall in any case. But since commencing this book, a useful treatise on Australian silver has appeared and, as a consequence, prices of native silver 'down under' have soared. As very few dealers in England would either recognise or bother about Australian silver the present situation offers obvious opportunities. The book is by Kurt Albrecht and published (1969) by Hutchinson Group (Australia) Pty Ltd, 30-32 Cremorne Street, Richmond, Victoria, Australia 3121 at $5.40. It is entitled *Nineteenth Century Australian Gold and Silversmiths*.

A few Australian dealers have already arrived here and are working round the shops and market stalls. They enquire for silver marked 'J.M. Wendt', this mark being either on its own or in conjunction with 'Adelaide' or various permutations of marks depicting a kangaroo, lion passant and anchor. The mark of H. Steiner, or with Steiner's initials (H.S. or H.ST.) is in equal demand. Again we have this name or initials, sometimes with the town mark, Adelaide, and at others with or without a crown, lion passant, kangaroo or even an emu. Kurt Albrecht's list of about forty known makers of Australian silver, extending from early in the nineteenth century to the beginning of the twentieth, reveals a rather uniform style in marking which may be *quite easily* recognised by collectors especially when the name of some Australian town is punched. The numerous and interesting illustrations in the same book show the typical over-decorated styles of Victorian England. Many of the more important items illustrated depict figures of aborigines, elaborate silver-mounted emu and ostrich eggs and an extensive use of the fern-leaf motif.

As it is not my intention to plagiarise a new book, I am passing on to you information gleaned from Australian dealers who have asked me to keep an eye open for their requirements. It has suited me to listen to them without making any promises.

Although I will not recommend Australian silver to collectors of fine antique silver, I do recommend your investment in Mr Albrecht's book if you wish to look around, find some examples and then earn an honest penny by selling your finds in their country of origin. It is pleasant to share a little 'inside information' with my readers.

Fashion, apart from mini-skirts and suchlike, can be a very boorish thing and although Australian silversmiths were generally inferior to their Victorian English counterparts, I have little doubt that Australian silver products are already more valuable than comparable English items.

In England an act in 1830 ('Jackson's' page 22) substituted transportation for the death penalty for those craftsmen who transgressed the law and forged the assay office marks. It may be mischievously amusing although unfair to suggest that criminal silversmiths deported from England probably contributed to the fraudulence rife amongst Australian jewellers and silversmiths in the boom days of the Australian gold rush in the middle of the nineteenth century. From the end of the nineteenth century there was prolonged lobbying by influential members of the very many honest Australian silversmiths to induce authority to control the industry by legislation, but nothing has come of these laudable efforts. In present times, in the continued absence of legislation, I hope and expect that a highly unsatisfactory situation has been resolved by enlightened common sense. .

14

Schedule of Study

This 'schedule of study' will seem, apart from the programme for the first two months, to constitute little more than an ever-increasing list of back-references, but these can be ignored if the reader will force himself to remember that most recommendations introduced in the early stages of the course should be practised and steadily perfected throughout the six months. The mere presence of these irritating references may serve to jolt the student's memory and save the necessity of constant repetition!

After an introductory first month of study, the remaining months are split into five quite distinct periods of antique silver starting with the Britannia Standard era (1697-1719), studying the rocaille vogue up to 1750 in the third month, continuing into the degeneration of the rococo decoration and the emergence of the styles inspired by the excavations at Pompeii in the fourth month, taking the first sixty years of the nineteenth century in the fifth and concluding with a study of very early silver. For each of these five months a list of museums, etc, is appended where a comprehensive selection of silver of the period under review may be studied.

It is my personal opinion that the order of study starts (months 2 and 3) and ends (month 6) with the very best that antique silver has to offer its students, but all periods, not excluding the much despised Victorian era, have much to interest and appeal to the connoisseur. Another purpose for starting specialised study with the Britannia Standard era is that the simplicity of design, the higher quality of silver and the above average robustness of most items of this period are all factors that tend to facilitate the recognition of good or bad patina.

In due course, the student may decide that from the middle of the eighteenth century the quality, design and craftsmanship of our silversmiths began to deteriorate. Despite the magnificent, if over-ornate creations of Paul Storr and several contemporary silversmiths at the outset of the nineteenth century, there seemed to develop both a sterility of inspiration and a lack of quality usually associated with mass-production. The voluptuously feminine designs of Hester Bateman (c.1780) are wholly desirable and much prized throughout the world, but the craftsmanship of some of her multitudinous staff and apprentices, in a factory seemingly geared for quantity rather than perfection and lacking perhaps stern masculine supervision, was certainly disappointing. The Victorian age, meeting the demands of a newly rich society, produced the maximum ostentation for the minimum cost and, as we have already remarked, was notorious for the pitiful ruination by fussy decoration of many fine examples of earlier and more aesthetic tastes.

This course must be a visual and palpable experience and I think you will enjoy it. You cannot learn much from the written word. In any case, it would be frustrating for you if I offered a bibliography because everything one recommends has the tiresome habit of being out of print and costly.

If you can acquire Sir C. J. Jackson's *An Illustrated History of English Plate* (2 vols:) and Charles Oman's *English Domestic Silver*, please do so.

You can and should obtain from your bookseller Sir Charles Jackson's *English Goldsmiths and Their Marks* and Frederick Bradbury's *British and Irish Silver Assay Marks* (your pocket guide to hall-marks and published by J. W. Northend Ltd, West Street, Sheffield 1). From the V & A Museum obtain Nos: 17, 24, 25, 27, 28, 29, 33, 37, 46 in their inexpensive *Small Picture Book* series. Above all, I recommend Eric Delieb's *Investing in Silver* published by Barrie & Rockliff and his *Silver Boxes* (Herbert Jenkins).

Those of my readers who live within easy reach of London and can find time to conduct their studies in the manner recommended should reach a stage of reasonable proficiency in our subject within the six months. Those living in remoter districts or overseas, may be severely handicapped in finding sufficient specimens to handle. In such circumstances, the problems may be resolved by each reader's individual initiative. One sound scheme is to suggest yourself as an unpaid assistant, whenever time permits, in a big shop specialising in silver.

Lack of sufficient important museum collections to inspect is not such a handicap, for an even greater activity with the scrapbook (see CI of this section), could be even more helpful if not as exciting.

FIRST MONTH:

AI. Go to a thoroughly reliable dealer, or take expert advice from Sotheby's or Christie's, and acquire one or more items of impeccable quality. Carry one such piece around with you in your pocket, taking care not to get it scratched or damaged. Acquire perfection and don't worry about price!

BI. Purchase large scrapbooks, a magnifying glass and the recommended books (para: 3 of this section).

CI. Acquire as many illustrations of antique silver as you can find —illustrated sales catalogues (from Christie's and Sotheby's, etc) and new and second-hand art magazines are good sources of supply—and paste them into your scrapbook, together with a brief description of each. All periods and as many styles as possible should be represented. Do not arrange your illustrations in any sequence of periods, but keep them well mixed up.

As soon as you have some twenty pages completed in your scrapbook, commence memorising or recognising the approximate date of every illustration. This is an important routine which should occupy at least an hour's study every day. By the end of the first month, supposing you have three hundred illustrations already pasted in, you should be able to open your scrapbook at any page and identify the period of every illustration at first glance.

DI. Make yourself familiar with the identification of assay and makers' marks in your 'Jacksons'.

EI. Visit as many collections, exhibitions and auctions of antique silver as time will permit. Try to date every item you see before checking with your descriptive catalogue.

FI. Handle as many items as possible and check them all with the routine inspection recommended in chapter 15 (part 2).

GI. As you learn to recognise the numerous conditions of patina by comparing all silver with your specimen example (AI), keep a watch for silver which has been electro-plated, and for items which have been dull-polished after recent repairs. The former condition sometimes affords a reasonable looking patina at first glance, but mellowness and depth of colour is missing and the touch seems sticky, with the impressions of finger-marks being noticeably more pronounced than on unrestored surfaces. Silver which has been dull-polished is distinctly dull in appearance.

The comparison between antique and very recent gilding is so obvious that you will not encounter initial difficulty in this respect. Modern gilding is harsh in appearance. Modern fire-gilding, producing a much softer and attractive colour, is rare and costly and the process can nowadays be undertaken only by special licence (it can be damaging to the health of craftsmen performing it).

As recent gilding almost invariably conceals repairs, it is good training to try and discover the exact purpose of the gilding.

Undue exception need not be taken to items which have been re-fire-gilt many years ago.

SECOND MONTH: Concentrate studies on Period 1690-1719.

A2. Continue schedules CI, EI, FI, GI.

B2. Inspect collections at Victoria & Albert Museum, Hampton Court, Ashmoleum Museum, Oxford, and auction rooms. Silver is on view at Christie's and Sotheby's for at least two clear days before the sales and these galleries do not close during luncheon hours. But the galleries are closed during August and September.

C2. Begin taking a keen interest in auction sales, they are your only criterion of prices. At the outset they will be unintelligible and even when you are competent to appreciate fully the items under consideration, you will still have to exercise your cunning and imagination.

Paradoxically, an expert on antique silver is not necessarily an expert of its valuation, but there are a few dealers, experienced in all aspects of our subject in constant attendance at the big, London auction rooms. You will soon get to know them by name because of their numerous purchases. These gentlemen will assist you tremendously, albeit unwittingly!

You are unlikely to learn much about prices at unimportant, provincial auctions. Here, there is usually insufficient expertise and financial backing to challenge the local 'ring', who often co-operate with the London 'ring'. For some items, the 'ring', either for the purpose of diverting attention from their illegal activities or to prevent an outsider from getting a bargain, will bid, even amongst themselves for the sake of added reality up to a realistic price. But they will hope to buy some of the better items very cheaply. The prices obtained for trivial items at auctions are equally unreliable. Two jealous housewives at 'daggers drawn' or inexperienced, overexcited dealers will often bid far above a realistic price. In such circumstances, I recall a late Georgian, fiddle pattern, pair of sugar tongs (worth about £3) reaching £28 before one of the contestants, fearful lest the laughter rippling through the tent was uncomplimentary, dropped out.

In London, because of opposition from knowledgeable private collectors and several unattached big dealers, the 'ring' is comparatively ineffectual and prices are often predictable.

The best advice that I can offer to the student of prices is to note the last bid (not necessarily successful) by a very experienced dealer. Record such bids together with your personal assessment of the lots concerned and when such notes are reasonably comprehensive use them to assist in your inspection prior to the sale. Continual comparison between your estimates and the actual prices obtained is your quickest route to efficiency. But remember that enquiry into the reasons for wide discrepancies will teach you far more than the satisfaction from your accurate prognostications. All this requires resolution and I wish that I had practised at the outset what I now preach.

If, after inspecting items at auctions, you are unable to attend the sale, ask the auctioneers to send you a list of prices obtained and names of purchasers. At Christie's and Sotheby's, catalogues and price lists can be sent to you for the entire season (October-July) for an inclusive fee.

D2. Try and spot items which have received later decoration: (1) In the period 1755-1770; (2) In the period c.1880.

E2. Examine the form of hinges of boxes.

THIRD MONTH: Concentrate on Period 1719-1750.

A3. Carry on with schedules C1, E1, F1, G1, C2, D2, E2.

B3. Visits to V & A Museum and auction rooms.

C3. Start trying to assess values of items inspected in accordance with suggestions outlined in chapter 12 (sec: b).

FOURTH MONTH: Concentrate on Period 1751-1800.

A4. Carry on with schedules CI, EI, FI, GI, C2, E2, C3.

B4. Visits to V. & A. Museum and auction rooms.

C4. Make a careful study of the styles in vogue (viz: bead and feather edges, bright-cut engraving, pierced sides, etc) so that you will recognise Victorian embellishments, in imitation of these late 18th century styles, on the many plain designs created in this and other periods.

D4. When handling silver, start routine check as detailed in part 1 of chapter 15.

FIFTH MONTH: Concentrate on Period 1800-1860.

A5. Carry on with schedules: CI, EI, GI, C2, D2, E2, D4.

B5. Visits to Ashmoleum Museum, Oxford, and auction rooms.

C5. Try and spot the numerous items in shops and auctions that have been de-chased.

SIXTH MONTH: Concentrate on Periods Prior to 1690.

A6. Carry on with schedules: CI, EI, GI, C2, D2, E2, D4, C5.

B6. Visits to British Museum, Knole Park, Windsor Castle, Messrs Christie's and Sotheby's.

15

Routine Inspection of Silver

This routine of selectivity is obviously unsuitable for those dealers catering for inexperienced customers and wishing to 'turn an honest penny' on all opportunities offered; and much of it is far too advanced for those of my readers who have been unable to complete lesson 13.

Rules:

1. Satisfy yourself concerning the patina and condition of item.
2. Estimate date of item.
3. Satisfy yourself regarding (a) design and (b) craftsmanship.
4. Satisfy yourself regarding weight for size and apply gentle pressure all over to ascertain if there is any thinness of metal or weak patches.

At this stage, you will have rejected the vast majority of antique plate inspected, but if you still remain reasonably satisfied:

5. Check hall-marks (if any) with your conclusion (rule 2). If there is a discrepancy of more than five years from either extremity of your estimated period, you will decide that the item is one of three things:

(a) A pioneer style—which is both interesting and suspicious.

(b) A reproduction or replacement item—which is not so interesting.

(c) A forgery. This, in view of your reasonable satisfaction after the implementation of the first four rules, is extremely unlikely. If a very clever forgery is suspected, re-check first three rules and examine for transposed, inserted or imitation hall-marks.

If the item is not a forgery:

6. Satisfy yourself about condition of marks and see that all moveable or attached parts (viz: lids and handles of tankards, etc) are marked and that all sets of marks coincide in every detail. If one or more of such parts be unmarked, check its patina very carefully with the rest of item. If there is a discrepancy of patina and no evidence of a repair, consider if the unmarked section could be a replacement. If it should be a replacement, I expect you will reject it unless it be of exceptional antiquity, historical importance and/or rarity.

7. Satisfy yourself that Coats of Arms, crests, initials and monograms are contemporary. During the six-month-course you will have instinctively absorbed a good knowledge of the heraldic designs, etc, in vogue in all periods. If there are no devices engraved, or occasionally applied, one must conclude that they have been removed unless the patina is really exceptional. Re-check on rule 4.

8. In the light of your conclusions, estimate value of item in accordance with suggestions of chapter 12 (sec: b).

Warnings.

Never allow yourself to be rushed or bullied during your inspection.

If you are handling an item from which some symbol of identification has been crudely obliterated, you are likely to be inspecting stolen property.

Routine Inspection.

PART 2.

In this second section we will consider a number of items and demonstrate a routine search for faults. This is a highly important part of the book and it has two purposes:

A. Like part 1, it has already been used extensively in chapter 14. In the years ahead, it can serve as a refresher course should one feel that one is getting slack and making small mistakes through over-confidence.

It is commonplace for the experienced to miss a small repair on some attachment to an article—such as a foot or handle—for it may be virtually insulated, so far as the repairers' processes are concerned, and the patina is destroyed on so small a proportion of the surface that it is difficult to spot in some lights. Such repairs, too, may have been stuck with 'Araldite' (or something similar) or neatly soldered with lead and neither of such repairs would have necessitated the application of intense heat and the ruination of the patina.

B. This section should provide considerable assistance to those readers who were unable to complete chapter 14. It must be assumed that such readers can at least recognise extremes of patina and, if unable yet to differentiate between contemporary and subsequent decoration, have decided to concentrate on items of simple, well-known design.

Reject: (a) Later decoration.
          (b) Electro-plated items.
          (c) Items with poor patina.
          (d) Items with recent gilding.

Continue: Apply gentle pressure over entire surface as you check for weak spots.

Breathe over surface to detect repairs and insertions.

Examine all areas of open-work silver with utmost care.

Check the junction of appendages to main body very carefully and make sure that the appendages are not damaged.

Examine all parts (especially the rims of salvers and trays, etc) against the light to spot small, unrepaired holes.

Beginners should be assisted in the early stages of their routine inspection by studying the risks pin-pointed in the diagrams and text as we examine a number of articles that collectively are reasonably typical of the whole field of our subject.

A. Check if handle of teapot is original.

B. Lid often breaks away from hinge. It is then usual to repair by adding an additional piece of silver on hidden surface to support juncture of lid and hinge.

C. Silver leafage at foot of this ivory knop might be snapped in places.

D. Look for a mark on lid of teapot (it may be only a lion passant) and see that such mark(s) check with duplicate(s) on body (with this style of pot, the full set of marks would be found on the base).

FIGURE 3. *A four-piece tea set dated circa 1795.*

E. Junctures on the teapot of spout with body and handle with body have often suffered repairs.

F. On teapot stand: legs may be broken off body and the legs may have been broken as well.

G. Look for signs of repairs (both inside and outside) at junctures of base and body of teapot and milk jug.

H. Look for splits (hold against the light) or repairs on rim of tea-pot stand, especially where the rim joins the flat surface of body.

I. All protruberances (such as flutes) and edges are subject to more wear than other parts and should be inspected very carefully.

J. Frequently, the end of the spout has been buckled and split. The spout may have been cut right down, even as far as an inch, and such a repair spoils the line of teapot.

K. Rims of milk jugs and sugar baskets are subject to splits.

L. Junctions of body to handle of a milk jug have often been repaired.

M. Frequently, an oval or circular patch has been inserted or applied to strengthen the junction.

N. The handle of a milk jug may have been snapped and repaired with 'Araldite'.

O. Swing handles should be marked with lion passant.

P. Other danger spots.

REPEAT WARNING.

There may be weak patches on one or all of the four items where heraldic devices or initials have been removed. Alternatively, there may be a patch applied over a weak spot to strengthen it or a patch inserted into body for same purpose.

A. It may seem simple enough to hammer out a dent or twist on this type of foot on mugs, castors, coffee pots, etc, but in doing so there is a high risk of the foot splitting and thus requiring a major repair. Sometimes, the repairer has thought it best to replace the original foot with a new one.

B. Rims are very liable to splits.

C. Junctions of handle with body need careful inspection.

D. Occasionally, the handle has been removed from its original position and replaced on another part of the mug to protect/conceal a weak patch. Do not forget to check this point.

E. The Victorians may have cut a triangle at point E and, by adding a spout turned the mug into a jug. In modern times, the spout is likely to have been removed and the jug turned back into a mug. If the replacement patch of silver is assayed with modern hall-marks, the 'new' mug is not an offending piece.

F. A false base with clear hall-marks may have been soldered over the original base. If one cannot see a faint outline of the punched marks from the inside of mug, check very carefully for this type of forgery.

FIGURE 4. *A silver mug.*
POINTS FOR ROUTINE INSPECTION

BOXES

Containers of most types are very popular with collectors. As many, such as counter-boxes, nutmeg-graters, patch-boxes, pomanders, snuff-boxes and vinaigrettes, were often carried in daily use throughout the lives of their owners, before they became collectors' pieces, a few carefully retained in cases but the majority of them jangling around in pockets or suspended from chains, we find comparatively few boxes that have escaped damage or hard wear. Obviously, we expect to find damage to hinges, corners and edges on oblong or similar forms of boxes, and much wear to engraved decoration on circular designs, that spend most of their time rolling around.

Many vinaigrettes have lost their delicate grilles and have either had replacements fitted, or the grille hinge fixtures have been removed and the erstwhile vinaigrettes are sold now as snuff or patch boxes. These alterations, together with repairs to box hinges and corners, etc, are usually concealed by gilding over. Unless the grille is very delicate, almost of filigree design, it should normally bear either a lion passant, a maker's mark or both.

Nutmeg graters have soared so high in value that we should expect a spate of forgeries at any moment.

Many of the earlier snuff boxes are either unmarked or bear only a makers' mark. Modern restorers are active in acquiring broken boxes, beyond repair, and converting this debris into complete, saleable units. Often these creations are attractive and it is an interesting game trying to determine the origins and periods of the components. Sometimes, we spot a fine Stuart lid, complete with contemporary coat, inserted into the lid-frame of a mid-Georgian box with a French mother-of-pearl or tortoiseshell body. The possible permutations of these 'marriages' are too numerous to list!

The demand for vinaigrettes and snuff boxes of the 'castle top' and kindred varieties with repoussé plaques inserted into lids with raised edges has produced one modern forger of some skill and knowledge. He cuts out a scene of Windsor Castle, for example, from a hitherto unsaleable visiting-card case and inserts it on to a flat lidded box with raised edges made in the appropriate period and by one of the well-known makers of these repoussé tops. As a result of all this hectic activity, even card cases have become quite valuable and I expect the forger will now switch to casting tops from an original repoussé design, probably by Nathaniel Mills. The forger's craftsmanship is far below the quality of Mills, Francis Clark, Joseph Willmore and Ledsam, Vale and Wheeler, and the plaques invariably seem to be inserted a trifle out of true, but this forger is making money.

CUPS, PORRINGERS, ETC

Many of the handles of such articles are replacements. Most of these vessels have lost their lids but may be none the less attractive for this.

MEAT SKEWERS

Some of these items have been mutilated either by being shaped into letter-openers or by being shortened to tidy up the point of skewer.

SALT CELLARS

These are frequently paper thin in the base due to frequent cleaning to remove corrosion.

SPOONS AND FORKS

Spoons become worn in the bowl; sometimes the shank snaps or cracks. Of the two repairs, the re-shaping of the bowls must be the more serious. The altered bowl is no longer representative of its period and, as an antique, it becomes almost as ridiculous as a berry spoon. I have seen early spoons (prior to eighteenth century) with half or more of a new bowl, in the correct shape, replacing the original worn-out part. It is wiser to leave a worn bowl as it is. Early spoons with knops such as apostle or seal top retain traces of gilding in the recesses of these designs. Knops are liable both to damage and loss of parts such as a nimbus or emblem from an apostle top. Sometimes the knop has broken from the stem and been resoldered. Most if not all London spoons have their knops joined to the stem by a V insertion, while most provincial spoons are connected with an L junction. Collectors are urged to make a special study of early spoons, after the completion of their present course, before risking any considerable financial outlay on them.

The tines of forks start deteriorating noticeably after about fifty years of constant use. In consequence, Georgian dessert forks, being more fragile than table forks, have become very rare indeed. Dessert spoons have been re-shaped into dessert forks very extensively and these forgeries can be identified by the flatness and lack of normal rigidity of the tines. As 'Old English' pattern tableware is more popular than the plain, 'fiddle' pattern, the shortage of 'O.E.' forks has been further eased by re-shaping dessert forks of the latter style. These alterations provide an obviously unsatisfactory version of the 'O.E.' design.

Caddy-spoons suffer the same troubles as larger spoons. The shovel types, probably used more often for sugar than for tea leaves, often appear with strange substitute handles to replace the original ivory or turned wood handles. Care should be taken when buying caddy spoons of the expensive Jockey-Cap variety. Large specimens bearing Hester Bateman's mark inside the crown are highly suspect. It is believed in authoritative quarters that these crowns were originally watch-cases of the mid 1770-80's, with modern peaks added and mock bright-cutting enrichment. Careful research has revealed that the smaller spoons marked inside their crowns, usually in a 'cross-formation', and normally by Joseph Taylor of Birmingham are perfectly genuine. Similarly, Jockey-Cap caddy spoons originating in London with marks in a straight line along the front or underside of the peak are genuine also. At one time, all Jockey-Cap caddy spoons unless marked on the side of the crown were considered suspect. Nevertheless, these are articles that the beginner should purchase only from reputable sources.

SUGAR TONGS AND NIPPERS

They require careful inspection. The centre of the U turn is a danger spot for tongs. The pierced tongs, constructed in three parts, usually have repairs or cracks down the pierced sides.

WINE LABELS

These popular little items have often been re-engraved with a more useful or popular title such as 'whiskey'. Pieces of borders on fragile, irregular designs have sometimes been broken. Such defects are often difficult to spot.

16

'Sheffield Plate' and How Genuine Pieces may be Recognised

'Sheffield Plate' deserves as much understanding as do Sheffield people. Its erstwhile vicissitudes, whilst prosperity ebbed or flowed, is over now, and in their relaxation from worry all the inherent kindness and consideration of north country folk sparkles, like many lights on all of Sheffield's hills and valleys to guide and greet the stranger in their midst. Even the harsh factories in this great industrial centre seem to have mellowed now, as if responsive to this human warmth, and press less heavily upon a stranger's thoughts. But the people still demand good value for their money, still retain their strength of character and if a complacent southerner displays rough manners their tolerance will soon wear thin and he will wish that he had never ventured north. This toleration, thin though it is, just like the silver surface of even their finest antique plate, is a precious treasure and must never be abused. It should be handled with soft gloves, as carefully as when inspecting an egg in a rare bird's nest, for once it is destroyed it is gone for ever. After many years, I have reached a proper understanding of this city and its much abused yet famous product. I've learned to love the finer specimens of 'Sheffield Plate' and to derive amusement from its worst examples.

Sheffield developed from a few scattered villages sheltering in the forests of Hallamshire, a district rich in coal and iron. In Elizabethan days this township with two thousand souls was famous not only for the making of cutlery but also, according to Hunter's 'History of Hallamshire' for some of the most beautiful parks and gardens in the country. The terrain nearby, whipped by gales and snowed under during much of the winter, with torrential waters (that also turned the cutlers' grindstones) rushing down the wooded slopes from the moors, must have bred a dour community. Sympathetic to the wild beauty of their environment, hospitable and kind behind a brusque exterior toughened by combat with the elements, they would invariably have called a spade a spade.

In 1743, the year in which the process of plating silver was discovered, the population of Sheffield was still less than ten thousand and the cutlery industry was possibly experiencing some difficulty.

Thomas Boulsover was repairing the handle of a knife composed of copper and silver when he had the good fortune to fuse the two metals accidentally. From this unusual clumsiness he realised it was possible to coat copper with silver, and, appreciating some of the commercial possibilities of his discovery commenced to manufacture a number of small items. The main significance of this discovery was the fact that once the two metals were fused together they would elongate in complete unison if rolled out in a sheet. Not all metals if fused like this would behave similarly.

Boulsover did not grow rich from his invention. He had too many other mechanical interests to concentrate his thoughts upon just one of them and he failed to realise that, whereas the majority of his potential customers might still prefer and could afford a solid silver button to a plated one, the profitable future for his invention lay in the reproduction of imposing items, which, because of their high cost when wrought from solid silver, were suitable only for those of high rank and considerable wealth.

Undoubtedly Boulsover was a brilliant mechanic and if he had perfected his invention before trying to market his immature products, thus revealing his secret, he might have reaped the early rewards. Eventually, he made money from making saws.

Perhaps Joseph Hancock was born lucky. It is considered probable that he was descended from the Hancocks of Ripley, near Eyam. If this is so, the burial register at Eyam suggests that he was lucky to be born at all for seven members of his father's family died of the plague between August 7th and August 10th, 1666.

Hancock saw Boulsover's invention, he improved upon it and

then commenced the manufacture of imposing items of good design. He was shrewd enough to realise that he had two types of potential customers from all parts of Europe: some he would please by enabling them to stock their silver boards, and thus ape their betters, and to others he could offer the more worthy joy of acquiring beautiful possessions within their means. Hancock prospered, new companies began manufacture, and craftsmen from afar flooded to the flourishing industry. Sheffield opened her arms to receive them.

Although fact or family loyalties induce me to believe that Jessop's Sheffield steel is the finest in the world, I have not always admired the city itself, and only after I had seen the entire centre of the city flattened by Nazi bombers did I learn to respect the calibre of its people. At first I was disturbed by its grime and size and then, as I grew older, because of its ruthless business acumen, as exemplified by the mass of horrific, busy factories and worried-looking, drab workers hurrying to their shift or lounging, apathetic and tired, in the public houses or on street corners—'liable to turn your car over if the home side lost at football,' I was told—I was reluctant to accept that either art or quality could emanate from such a source. Because of this irrational prejudice, shared by not a few, and still forgetful of the town's more peaceful origins, it was a long time before I could accept that some antique silver assayed at Sheffield and a considerable quantity of Sheffield Plate is of a high order of craftsmanship and that some of both is truly beautiful.

'Sheffield Plate' originated as a reasonably priced substitute for silver and in consequence was not always cherished or respected, but I have now seen examples of it as sensuous of line as anything designed by Hester Bateman, as original in conception as anything created by Paul Lamerie or Paul Storr, and although most styles ran behind in slightly later imitation of designs in vogue with goldsmiths, and very occasionally of the Leeds potters as well, there are rare instances when the precedence was reversed and silversmiths were not too proud to imitate the platers. Above all other considerations in the appraisement of our current subject, I can assure my readers that the beauty of the patination on some fine old plate is unsurpassed even by the best Elizabethan examples in silver. The unfortunate but inevitable tragedy of 'Sheffield Plate' is that the thin sheets of silver covering the copper are sadly vulnerable to wear and damage and thus comparatively few examples survive in pristine state. If we are fortunate enough to find worthy specimens within our means, we should never consider them as antique silver's poor relations. Sheffield Plate must be highly prized and most *carefully preserved*.

FIGURE 5. *A Leeds pottery jug imitated in 'Sheffield Plate', circa 1790.*

My first visit to Sheffield at the age of eight, shortly after my father's death—he had never fully recovered from being blown up in Gallipoli—involved a memorable and at first a dreary drive through a drizzle from east to west of the city and then out to a relative's shooting-box high on the moors beyond sight, sound and smell of industry. As we climbed a rough stone road away from so-called progress, blue patches of sunlit sky divided the gloom of darkened clouds and split the vast, heather-clad wolds into thrilling segments of dark or vivid purple.

After our arrival, at about five-thirty I should think, even the tea-table overflowing with delectable 'scoff' could not avert my occasional glances through the window. It was the arrival of roast grouse with full accessories that surprised me beyond all thoughts of scenic delights. 'Good heavens,' I said to myself with glee, for I was a greedy child, 'if afternoon tea is such a feast, what on earth lies in store for dinner?' The prospects were so exciting that I ate sparingly for I sensed that even *my* seemingly insatiable appetite was about to be challenged. At about six-thirty, while we were still sitting round the tea-table, I asked if it was time to go to my room to change. Discipline of those bygone days, when for special occasions or as a guest I was allowed to stay up for dinner, decreed that I should wear my Eton suit with its uncomfortably high, stiff collar.

'Changed for what?' my hostess asked.

'For dinner, Cousin Gertrude,' I replied.

It was my elder sister who recovered first from the surprise of my wishful thinking. 'The little pig,' she exclaimed.

'What a greedy child,' Cousin Gertrude remarked sternly from the head of the table, 'has he got worms?'

Although my poor mother, with a laugh that was palpably forced, explained that it was my first visit to Yorkshire and that I had never before experienced a high tea, it was a terrible moment for a child who was both sensitive and greedy. And worse; by now the grouse had been removed.

This was my first encounter with the realism of Sheffield people: these folk, even if well-to-do, who managed on three meals a day instead of four and who called a worm a worm even at a tea table in 1921, would not bother about the traditional respect for a precious metal if they could produce an acceptable substitute at a much less cost and thereby make a load of 'brass'. Of course, 'Sheffield Plate' was bound to spring from such people.

Just as the recent boom in the interest for antique silver has attracted a large number of new dealers, many of whom we welcome while some others we deplore, the new industry at Sheffield also presented serious problems soon after its inception. Plate was in ready demand both in England and overseas and the bonanza must have got out of control. An extract taken from a paper written by Arnold Watson, a Master of the Sheffield assay office towards the end of the last century, is worth recording here. Even if the information given to Mr Watson was considerably exaggerated there are still grounds for thinking that there was both a shortage of skilled labour and dishonest practices yielding high profits if we consider the value of money in the eighteenth century in proportion to the amount of the holiday loans quoted:

'I am told that it was no uncommon thing for men in a shop to demand £50 or £100 to support them whilst they went "on spree"; and one instance has been given in which a party of seven braziers who had been absent for a week (upon money already advanced by their master) sent two of their number for a further £10 each, to be added to their individual debts, on which condition only they promised to return to work the following week; and this condition was complied with.'

But there were other craftsmen, usually unskilled with anything but their hands, who stinted and saved and then set up in business on their own account. Whilst admiring their enterprise one wonders if they were responsible for most of the very thinly plated examples of this industry. In this same paragraph, we can draw attention to the forgery of coins of the realm. With skilled engravers at Sheffield and Birmingham, this development could have been expected. Needless to say, it was only silver coins of higher denomination that were reproduced and as it was a difficult process, usually involving the use of a white base metal (which helped to conceal the deceit when the silver plate wore thin), the currency was never seriously threatened. Surviving examples of these counterfeit coins are very rare.

Further evidence pointing to malpractices at the two main centres of the industry is to be found in the concern expressed by London goldsmiths regarding the marks punched by platers on their wares. The public had no pocket guide to assay office hall marks in those days and in all likelihood accepted any set of symbols or initials as denoting sterling silver. Advantage was taken of this ignorance. The goldsmiths' agitation was probably as justified as it was certainly prolonged. It was not until 1773, and in the actual Act of Parliament establishing an assay office at Sheffield, that platers were forbidden to punch their wares with marks. But an act of 1784 permitted the resumption of marks on Sheffield Plate and indeed it tried to control the industry by requiring (even if optimistically) each maker of plate working within a hundred miles of Sheffield to register his mark at the Sheffield silver assay office.

Readers who wish for detailed information concerning the processes involved in the manufacture of Sheffield Plate or who wish to make a more advanced study of the industry as a whole, are advised to procure Thomas Bradbury's *History of Old Sheffield Plate* reprinted in 1969 by Messrs J. W. Northend Ltd of Sheffield.

The base metal used in the production of Sheffield Plate was predominantly copper but combined very small quantities of either zinc or lead. The silver employed was usually of the sterling standard. This combination produced a temper that was neither too soft nor too brittle for fashioning. From about 1830, German silver (see glossary) was frequently used as a base metal and this had the advantage of not showing through so obviously when the silver became worn.

Boulsover made his ingots—prior to rolling them into sheets from which he fashioned his wares—by fusing just one layer of silver to one bar of copper. This process, of course, left one side of his plated sheet devoid of silver. He tinned the interiors of his boxes, buttons and similar small things, and this not only gave the appearance of silver to a cursory glance when the objects were new, but also prevented the otherwise exposed copper from corroding or staining everything that came in contact with it. In the nineteenth century it was still quite a normal practice for platers to economise by producing large articles such as trays with tinned bases.

In the early days of the industry, if it was required to have a silver coating on both sides of an object then two ingots of Sheffield Plate, plated on one side only, were soldered together. From about 1760, ingots made from *single* bars of base metal, plated on both sides, seem to have been in normal production and the method of manufacture did not vary. One bar of base metal was sandwiched between two sheets of silver and these were of equal breadth and length and were thoroughly filed, planed and cleaned. Two outer copper sheets were then positioned to protect the two silver surfaces when the ingot was heated and a coating of borax prevented them from fusing to the ingot. Thus, before fusing there were five bars or sheets and these were tightly bound together: 1. A protective sheet of copper (prevented from fusing to the ingot). 2. A sheet of silver. 3. A bar of copper. 4. A sheet of silver. 5. A protective sheet of copper. The resulting ingot was from about 1½″ to 5½″ deep by 2½″ wide, and its length was made suitable to the particular projects in view. The ingot's content of silver, if of good quality, represented about five to eight per cent of the whole; but much Sheffield Plate was made with a very much smaller proportion of the precious metal. Finally, the ingot was drawn out by rollers or forge hammers into a sheet of the requisite size and thickness. The rollers were at first pulled by hand, but, once the industry was established, they were replaced by water-power.

Hollow plated wire was used for edges in the seventeen sixties, and from 1768 solid plated wire was used. In 1789, Messrs Roberts and Cadnam began soldering silver wire and silver borders upon lips, edges and bases, areas exposed to heavy wear and early exposure of copper, and so it became possible to ornament plate successfully with gadroon and beaded borders, and similar attractive vogues of that time. Various other refinements were introduced by individual platers (the firm of Roberts and Cadnam continuing to be responsible for new ideas) until the advent of electro-plating invented in 1837 soon terminated the manufacture of Sheffield Plate.

Towards the end of the nineteenth century, some fifty years after the manufacture of true Sheffield Plate had ceased, collectors commenced buying examples of the 'dead' industry and by the turn of the twentieth century it had become more valuable than contemporary sterling silver and this fact, of course, led to the mass production of imitation Sheffield Plate. Copper articles fashioned in an approximation of antique styles were electro-plated and some manufacturers stamped the words Sheffield Plate upon their products. Dealers were within their rights in selling these spurious reproductions so long as they did not describe them as antique in their sales patter.

But the public had much cleverer forgeries to contend with then and the position is still very dangerous today. Sheets of Sheffield Plate, ready for fashioning, may still be bought, and I am told that there is one dealer who boasts that much of the Sheffield Plate currently passing through the sale rooms was made by his father—copying the authentic, original processes—at the beginning of this century. But this claim is considered to be greatly exaggerated.

The argument that reproducers of antique plate, made by the authentic, original processes satisfy a popular demand merely because they are more durable than electro-plated articles, cannot be upheld. The anonymity of Edwardian and modern reproductions is clear evidence of an intention to deceive the public. Bona-fide manufacturers reproducing Sheffield Plate would identify themselves with a trade mark and would number or even date their products.

Although these reproductions are so far confined to popular items such as trays, candlesticks, chambersticks, pots, bowls and jugs, the ability to recognise antique patination seems the first essential before a collector embarks on purchases without expert assistance.

Provided that antique plated ware has been cherished by all of its several owners, most of it that was fashioned from sheets with thick silver plate is usually, apart from a few inevitable scratches, more beautiful today than when it was made because of its delightful patination easily recognisable by its blue-grey tint.

Another abuse of Sheffield Plate still flourishing openly today and which ruins much genuine old plate, is the electro-plating with new and garish silver (which is usually very thinly applied) of items that by reason of honest hard wear revealed too much copper for the public's taste. Alas! the customer is usually wrong. Antique plate after being electro-plated—a very different process of silvering copper —automatically ceases to be authentic Sheffield Plate. Unless you are purposely making a collection of silver-ware that has been ruined by restoration (an interesting hobby, perhaps, but generally unrewarding as an investment) it is much wiser to spurn all re-plated items.

After the boom of the late Victorian and Edwardian eras in both genuine and spurious plate, most erstwhile customers eventually considered that they had been duped, and the bottom fell out of the market, to the delight of a few fully experienced collectors. Today, I suppose, after some revived interest, genuine antique plated ware averages about a fourth or a fifth of the cost of its antique silver counterpart.

I am certain that less than ten per cent of the plate sold as Sheffield Plate today is genuine. This deplorable situation springs both from the usual sources of ignorance and wishful thinking, and also because Sheffield Plate has become a trade term for any item of silvered copper even if made in Mecca! There are, however, good and interesting examples of genuine, continental Sheffield Plate made in the eighteenth and nineteenth centuries. Such pieces often copy English styles and unless the item under inspection is a samovar, for example, it is often very difficult to determine the country of origin.

Tomasina, nearly eighty years old and as gay as a grig, was a remarkable character and seemed unnecessarily generous for trade. If she mistakenly sold a piece of spurious plate that was subsequently returned to her, she would not only refund any purchase price claimed (whether she had originally sold the piece or not, one suspected) but would request the customer to keep the item in compensation for his disappointment. One heard strange fragments of conversations at her stall, quite possibly on the following lines:

'That's only five,' Tomasina might say, quoting a price and thinking in shillings.

'Well, I'll offer you four pounds ten.'

'Four pounds ten?' echoed Tomasina in amazement, 'why, dear, it's only five shillings.'

'Then, I'll offer four and sixpence.'

How To Recognise *Genuine* Sheffield Plate:

We come now to the most important part of this chapter and in order that readers may refer to it quickly when occasion demands, it seems best to list the characteristics of Sheffield Plate concisely.

1. Patination: The blue-grey tinge on unrestored surfaces (so similar to good patination on antique silver) is very conspicuous when compared with surfaces that have been re-plated or otherwise ruined. If you can visit the City of Sheffield Museum at Weston Park, please do so without delay. You will be able to recognise the difference between good and bad patination with just one glance. I only hope that you will remember this difference. Turn left immediately on entering the hall containing the museum's exciting collection of Sheffield Plate. In the first case by the door and against the wall and on the second shelf from the top of the case there is a tankard mug that in my confident opinion has been re-plated on its body, but the handle was shielded from this process and has not been re-plated. Presumably, the piece is retained in the collection because of some special point of interest. I am told that the damage on the body which necessitated the re-plating was a large dent. It had to be hammered out and this damaged the original surface. There is always a *high risk* in attempted restoration of Sheffield Plate. The contrast between the colour of this mug and the exquisite blue-grey tones of all the other pieces on the same shelf is so marked that it must be spotted without difficulty by everyone, however inexperienced, providing that they are not colour-blind. This restored mug was the first item that caught my eye as I entered the hall. It *screamed* at me in a nasty raucous voice! This mug, such a splendid example of bad colour, can be seen very clearly through the glass of its case. Should this case have been re-arranged by the time you

get there, the number of the exhibit concerned is L.1943.142., and the curator will point it out on request.

It may be a chemical action produced by the copper or it may be the latter's obscure presence beneath the gradually thinning silver surface that provides Sheffield Plate with a patination rather more pronounced than on contemporary silver items.

2. Seams: Sheffield Plate is more difficult to raise from the flat than is silver and except for very shallow bowls and entrée dishes, for example, the metal has to be joined for the fashioning of all articles of depth. This junction is called a seam and it is clearly visible. If the seam has been covered recently by heavy re-plating, it may not be visible or it may be visible only in places. Look also for seams on knops, feet and handles.

3. Applied Rims, etc: Hollow plated wire was used on edges in the 1760's. From about 1768, further experiments were made by applying solid plated wire to edges. From about 1789, stamped out silver borders filled with lead solder were introduced. The eye can see and the thumbnail usually feel the junction of these various borders with the body of the item.

4. Bright-cut Engraving: This was possible on items made from ingots with thicker silver sheets. Sometimes we find solid silver bands, with bright-cut enrichment, soldered round the bodies of tea pots and so forth.

5. Hollow-ware: The interiors of tea and coffee pots, or any receptacle into which a guest's eye was unlikely to pry, were hardly ever plated by the Sheffield process, but I have seen such interiors that have been gilt.

6. Shields: Unless the plate was unusually thick, it was necessary for crests and monograms, etc, to be engraved on a silver shield, which was either inlaid (soldered in a hole cut right through the body-wall), rubbed in or soldered on. The inlaid shields date from about 1789 and rubbed in shields from about 1810.

7. Decoration In Relief: In the nineteenth century, when elaborate floral, vine and shell edges were in vogue, these were die-stamped from thin silver sheets and then filled with lead solder.

As with antique silver, the collector should inspect as many pieces of Sheffield Plate as possible, visit museums and exhibitions, and carry a small, carefully protected item—e.g. wine label—around with him for comparison.

17

Picture Quiz on Period Styles

A. *About 11 in tall.*

B. *About 9 in tall.*

FIGURE 6.

c. *About 12in tall.*

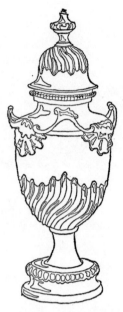

D. *About 6in tall.*

E. *About 5in tall.*

F. *About 5½in tall.*

FIGURE 6.

G. *About 15in wide.*   H. *About 18in in diameter.*

I. *About 5½in tall.*   J. *About 4½in tall.*

FIGURE 6.

K. *About 5½ in wide.*

L. *About 3½ in tall.*

M. *About 15 in wide.*

N. *About 6in tall.*

FIGURE 6.

Answers on page 118.

18

Idiosyncrasies

The dealer who is both sufficiently competent and genuinely anxious to help his customers takes a little finding. Such a dealer, eccentric and individualist as he may well be, will respond to warmth and charm and although he will differentiate immediately between a customer's tact and a real enthusiasm, will appreciate the former as much as the latter because it reflects good manners from nice people. Similarly, the dealer likes a customer to chat and admire the stock even when the possibility of a sale is not discussed. On this understanding, a mutual confidence will develop and the customer is assured of good service.

Unless you know a dealer extremely well, it is unfair to ask him for a valuation or an opinion on an item bought elsewhere. I am so frightened of being associated with the far too common practice of 'knocking' other traders' goods that I would not make any serious criticisms unless the item was a forgery. I would also overvalue goods brought to me for free valuation and thus my opinion is worthless.

A good dealer will be convinced that the silver he is offering represents sound investments and, contrary to the public's general conception of dealers as a whole, he may not be anxious to part with his more desirable pieces except to suitable customers. If the customer, whether he be collector or dealer, has purchased something from a trader in the past and does not think he is recognised on a subsequent visit, he would be wise to remind the dealer and to add how pleased he is with the previous purchase.

A customer, insensitive to an expert's desire to offer him good value, who states baldly and ignorantly that some treasure being examined is 'far too expensive' is asking to be snubbed discreetly by even the most kind and polite of dealers. The customer would be well advised to offer some tactful excuse for his disinterest. Few good dealers suffer fools gladly nor are they impressed by the ignorant or naïve who try to fault perfection in the hope of a reduction in price.

It is unwise to attempt to beat a good dealer down in price. Even if he was successful once, the dealer is unlikely to hold this type of customer in high esteem. In the antique business a trade discount is offered to dealers whenever possible and this concession may be extended in due course to regular approved customers. The type of dealer who is willing to conduct his business in the style of an Egyptian bazaar will not, unless by chance, stock good antique silver and he should be treated with the utmost circumspection even by the experienced.

Like most dealers in antiques I am fortunate with my customers and many of the most charming are members of the medical profession from every quarter of the globe and numerous trans-Atlantic dealers, but we do have to suffer a sprinkling of would-be thieves, confidence tricksters, irritating idiots and eccentrics.

'Is it sterling?' is a disappointing question when the speaker has spent the last ten minutes studying one's stock of antique silver with its descriptive notes. I have been known, when there seemed to be an aggressive patronage in this query, to play an equally obtuse part and derive some compensatory amusement from the questioner's subsequent bewilderment. 'From the Stirling assay office?' I ask with amazement, 'virtually, there is none to be found in all the world. Whatever makes you ask if this is Stirling silver— ... Oh! I understand now, you seek silver of the sterling standard, but wouldn't you prefer something rather better?' then, with a sniff, 'there's cheap and nasty alloy in the sterling quality, isn't there?'

If readers sometimes feel that their favourite dealer is aloof or moody, this could be caused by the frailty of human nature or it might be that the dealer has just received absorbing but unfortunate news; a dissatisfied customer, a dishonoured cheque, a theft from stock or a demand from a 'squeezed' bank to reduce an overdraft are all examples of irritations that may beset dealers. These moods may be more speedily removed, if illogically, by the acquisition of an interesting item of silver than by the arrival of a customer.

Confidence tricksters are particularly annoying because they make the dealer feel such a fool. Slight flaws in the performance of these talented actors become exaggeratedly obvious in retrospect.

A young couple came to see me on a Thursday and inspected a particularly fine Charles II box. They spoke as if they had bought things from me before. On the following day the couple sent a young man to inspect the box on their behalf and he informed me that he would not hesitate to recommend it very strongly. 'They'll probably come along to buy it, tomorrow,' he added.

On Saturday the couple re-appeared. 'We've come to have another look at the box,' the man began. Although I was pleased to see them, because they seemed a nice couple and I liked their enthusiasm, I failed to give them any lead to the closing of the sale because I was reluctant to lose so nice a box. In consequence, there developed about a half-hour's performance, probably rehearsed at the outset but, in retrospect, appearing a little laboured by the girl after the first few minutes as she waited for a pre-arranged signal from her boy friend before admitting her unquenchable desire to possess. Their act, consisting of numerous variations of the same theme, ran somewhat like this: 'It's such a lovely box, darling, I'm sure we would treasure it all our lives.' The girl replied: 'I love it too, beloved, but can we afford it?' Every now and then I interjected with further cautionary advice and the man must have hated me for it. Eventually, the rascal despairing of my co-operation, and fearful probably that his accomplice's theatrical talents were being overtaxed gave her the agreed signal and she responded: 'I do want it so much and as you're sure it's an investment we'd be silly to miss it. Please buy it.'

The man felt in his right-hand jacket pocket and withdrew, all in one hand and movement, a driving licence, banker's credit-card and cheque book. But this unusually neat production of documents did not seem suspicious at the time. Before I could inspect the card and the licence properly, if at all, my attention was somehow diverted, probably because I was rather touched by the man's thoughtfulness for my interests. 'I know you've had cheques from me before, Mr Luddington,' he said, 'but this one will be for an unusually large amount. Would you care to keep the box until my cheque is cleared?'

Reacting to this consideration in precisely the manner expected of me, I hastened to assure him that I had no doubts at all about his cheque. But I think I was aware at this stage, even if only subconsciously, that the girl was nervous.

The cheque was one from a stolen book, the name and address written on the back were fictitious of course and the box was sold cheaply three days later by the girl to a public company specialising in antiquities. The company maintains that in accepting a stolen cheque, I passed the lien of the box to the man. I disputed this view because I was induced to believe that the man was someone other (i.e. an old customer) than he in fact was. All this happened some years ago and I finally dropped the matter. Things might have been less complicated had the police or the public company informed me immediately when the box and confidence trick were discovered. This ordinary courtesy both parties forgot, presumably because of pressure of work, and it was left to me to find out by telephoning and enquiring of the police some six months after the couple had been arrested.

Kleptomania, often considered in our complex form of democracy to be a complaint exclusive to our upper classes, is of course prevalent also amongst our lower classes, but in these latter groups I believe it is called larceny! We can, however, all accept the distinction between compulsive and pre-meditated larceny and the inexperienced dealer is advised to prepare himself for these two emergencies in different ways. For both compassionate and commercial reasons there must always be grave doubts about the wisdom of prosecuting a kleptomaniac and there may even be occasions when it is best to ignore the theft. The following story does not illustrate all these points, but it may be of assistance to young dealers.

One of the greatest interests after Y's retirement was his pottering around the antique shops and markets. Obviously he had wealth, we all knew of his position and influence and above all he was a man one respected instinctively. He usually came alone—for I think his wife remained at their place in the country—and he always stopped to chat with or buy from me. I enjoyed all his visits except for one! He introduced me to his sons who were on holiday from school and shortly afterwards I met his wife. While her husband was selecting a modest piece of silver costing a few pounds, I saw her pick up a set of six Georgian table spoons and slip them into her bag.

On receiving payment for the husband's small purchase, instead of my saying 'then there are the spoons to pay for, aren't there?' I was foolish enough to look at the wife and ask inoffensively 'and are you taking anything else?' 'No, nothing more this time,' the husband interjected, but the wife said nothing, looked fidgety and began to move away. I had lost my opportunity and there was nothing to be done without embarrassing my friend and regular customer.

I never saw either of them again. Apparently the husband's interest in antique silver had suddenly ceased, but it is probable that he became suspicious, possibly because of a past history to his wife's kleptomania, and he, not knowing from whence the spoons came, felt to ashamed to be seen in his old haunts ever again.

I can imagine a conversation between husband and wife on the following lines:

'Where did these spoons appear from, dear, I haven't seen them before?'

'I picked them up very cheaply in the Portobello road.'

Personally, I fear that those spoons cost the couple a great deal of sorrow.

The most mystifying customer-performance was played by a rather scholarly looking gentleman. He made two visits in the course of a morning and spent a long time examining a Georgian sauce boat from all angles and with a curious intentness. Finally, whilst he was almost lying on the floor and seeming to peer through a glass shelf at the sauce boat's base, I asked him if he would like to handle the piece and examine the marks. My intrusion upon his thoughts seemed to cause embarrassment. 'No, no, not at all, thank you,' he replied, 'I must be going now ... an important lecture to deliver on the antipodes, you know.' Before struggling into a mackintosh and hustling off into a sun-soaked street, he did not forget his nice manners: 'thank you once again, I found your sauce boat of most absorbing construction. I have another at home exactly similar but of minor interest in comparison. You do realise, of course, that yours is upside down?'

Apart from unfortunate purchases—and it is the purpose of this book to prevent these—sad and unpleasant experiences in the pursuit of silver are rare. Silver has happy associations with the past, the present and the future. It is at its best by candlelight in the evening of your lives when work is done and great friends or their shadows sit with you around a splendid table. It blends so well with special glass and suitable apparel, with port and flowers and ancestors who watch from gilded frames, with repartee or serious talk and with a pretty daughter's décolleté. It blends with polished wood, stately mirrors and haughty rooms, with well-loved servants or their ghosts and everything that's loyal and true.

Perhaps and quite by chance we know at last how patina is best described. Is it the spirit of gracious living alight within the metal, which when transmitted down the generations—thus fanned continually by jealous care, admiring glances and a *soupçon* of magic—is recognised by you, my reader, and then enjoyed for life and finally passed on still further enhanced?

Summary.

This final section is short and sour. It offers two suggestions:

1. Regard everything as 'guilty' until you have proved it 'innocent'.

2. No responsible dealer should object to giving you a written guarantee of authenticity and a detailed, guaranteed, accurate statement of condition, listing all repairs and/or alterations, with every purchase. Ask your dealer for such a guarantee.

THE END OF THE BEGINNING

A customer is encouraging his children to take an interest in antique silver. At a recent 'fork-luncheon' every piece of silverware in the house was pressed into service. In the middle of the function, one of my customer's children examined his fork and piped up: 'I've got a letter "A" and a king's head on my fork.' Another guest, even younger, tried to follow suit but revoked: 'Mine's got "stainless steel made in Japan".'

Glossary

Unless you wish to indulge in some harmless intellectual snobbery it does not matter a scrap, so far as your ability to recognise and buy good silver is concerned, whether or not you know the difference between an aurifex and an aurifaber or, for further examples, if you can recognise a cavetto, fylfoot or triskele. But a mini-glossary may assist the student in his initial reading.

Arabesque.	Fanciful design of intertwined flowers, leaves and branches engraved in low relief.
Casting.	The pouring of molten metal into a mould of plaster. The model, usually made of wax, around which the plaster has been shaped, is dispelled by heat.
Chasing.	See embossing.
Cut-Card-Work.	A design cut from a sheet of silver and then soldered to another silver article.
De-Chasing.	The slow, expensive process of flattening embossed surfaces. Much antique silver with non-contemporary decoration has been hammered flat (de-chased) and thus restored ostensibly to its original form. Careful examination of this process when completed reveals traces of hammer blows and (usually) faint indications of incompletely removed decoration. The original patina is destroyed.

Die-Casting.	Silver impressed with a design from a steel die.
Electro-Gilding.	Mechanical, modern method of applying thin coat of gold upon silver. The result is neither durable nor of good colour.
Embossing.	Decoration in relief that has been hammered from the reverse side. Chasing: hammered from outside inwards.
Engraving.	Incised decoration.
Feather-edge.	Pattern of incised short lines at edge of flat-ware (spoons and forks, etc).
Filigree.	Designs in tracery formed by silver wire.
Finial.	An ornament at an extremity of an article.
Fire-gilding.	A mixture of gold and mercury applied on a silver surface. The mercury is then dispelled by heat while the gold combines with the silver. This method prevents tarnishing and combines a fine colour with durability.
Flat-chasing.	Decoration by depressing metal with a blunt tool.
Fluting.	Decoration by channels either convex or concave.
Gadrooning.	A series of short, convex, curved flutes.
German Silver.	A white alloy of nickel, copper and zinc.
Knop.	See finial.
Nimbus.	(when applied to silver spoons) The disk surmounting the figure on an apostle spoon.
Patina.	A word 'borrowed' by silver dealers and referring to the general appearance or colour of a silver surface.
Parcel-gilt.	Partly gilt.
Repoussé.	See embossing.
Rocaille (rococo).	A form of decoration in the taste of artificial rock and shell constructions at Versailles.
Stamped out.	See Die-Casting.
A runner.	A runner borrows stock on short-loan from a dealer and tries to sell it.
Under-bidder (the)	He who makes the penultimate bid at an auction. Sometimes called the 'runner-up'.

Answers to 'Period Styles' (See pages 106-109)
Illustration A: Circa 1770., B: 1720., C: 1795., D: 1760., E: 1680.,
F: 1710., G: 1820., H: 1750., I: 1705., J: 1740., K: 1745., L:
1780., M: 1840., N: 1695.

Index

Index